RELATIONSHIPS
ADULT CHILDREN OF ALCOHOLICS

OTHER BOOKS BY JOSEPH PEREZ

Coping within the Alcoholic Family, 1986

Counseling the Alcoholic Group, 1986

Counseling the Alcoholic, 1985

A Father's Love, 1982

Family Counseling: Theory and Practice, 1979

Family Roots of Adolescent Delinquency, 1978

Mom and Dad Are Me, 1969

General Psychology, 1968

The Initial Counseling Contact, 1968

Counseling: Theory and Practice, 1966

RELATIONSHIPS

Adult Children of Alcoholics

Joseph F. Perez, Ph.D.

GARDNER PRESS TRADE BOOK COMPANY

Library of Congress Cataloguing-in-Publication Data

Perez, Joseph F. (Joseph Francis)
    Relationships: adult children of alcoholics.

    Includes index.
    1. Adult children of alcoholics—United States.
2. Alcoholics—United States—Family relationships.
3. Interpersonal relations. I. Title. (DNLM:
1. Alcoholism—popular works. 2. Parent-Child
Relations—popular works. WM 274 P4377r]
HV5132.P47 1988   362.2'92   87-21105
ISNB 0-89876-150-6 (pbk.)

Gardner Press Distribution
c/o M. & B. Fulfillment Service
540 Barnum Avenue
Bridgeport, CT 06608
(203) 366-1900

Foreign orders, except Canada, South America, Australia, and New Zealand to:
        Afterhurst Limited
        27 Palmeira Mansions
        Church Road, Hove,
        East Sussex BN 3 2FA
        England

Orders for Australia and New Zealand to:
        Astam Books
        27B, Llewellyn Street
        Balmain, N.S.W., Australia

To Frank and Betty Bansfield
whose relationship
I treasure.

C O N T E N T S

A PREFACE

JEANIE'S STORY

"Lushes Die Alone!"

When I was in the third grade, I saw a lot of Jeanie Gordon. One reason I did so was that she was the only kid who lived within a three-block radius. But the main reason was probably that I was in charge of our relationship. I ordered her around. An only child, I had never been in any position to order anyone around. I still do not know if the experience was beneficial for my development and character. I do know I liked it; it fed my budding masculinity and gave me a sense of power.

My mother also liked Jeanie. She often asked her to stay for dinner. I attributed Jeanie's steadfast refusals to her shyness.

After school, Jeanie and I would go to my house to play. We seldom went to her house because I felt uncomfortable there. Her mother made me feel that way.

Mrs. Gordon was very fat, and she was moody. Moody was an adjective that seemed to fit virtually all the women in my life (my teacher, my Sunday School nun, and every other mother I knew, including my own). But Mrs. Gordon's moodiness, to my naive but exquisitely accurate eight-year-old interpersonal sense, was disconcerting. It was different.

Mad, sad, or glad, she made me very nervous. Once we came in to find her standing in the middle of the kitchen, gesticulating angrily, her face masked in hate, screaming at Mr. Gordon. She was so angry that she neither saw nor heard us.

She was using words that I had never heard from any mother. They were the kind I had only begun to hear at recess at the playground, the kind that were used only among males. We left.

The scene had so bewildered me that I was oblivious to Jeanie's embarrassment. Just how acute that embarrassment was became apparent on the way to my house. Never especially talkative, she suddenly started blabbering in a funny, choked-up way, as though tears had mixed with her words and were coming out of her mouth instead of her eyes. "When she gets like that, she gets like that for a long time. Sometimes for a whole day, until I go to bed, and sometimes she's like that the next day too . . ." She went on and on and on. Then shy, reticent Jeanie, who had never asked me for anything, asked, "Can I stay overnight?"

I sensed what that request had cost her, and that I was not supposed to discuss the real why of her staying over with my mother or father. I didn't. My mother cleared her stay with her father. Mrs. Gordon couldn't come to the phone. She was sick, he told her. And yes, Jeanie could stay over.

Another time when I accompanied Jeanie home, we found Mrs. Gordon alone and crying. I had never seen an adult cry. It unnerved me. Jeanie asked her what was wrong. Tears flowing, she wailed that she was lonely, that she had no friends, that no one liked her. Jeanie told her that she did. I echoed Jeanie's sentiment, but without much conviction. I left, embarrassed and very confused.

I remember feeling guilty as I walked home, convinced that the weakness of my reassurance had caused her to continue her wailing.

She repeated this sad scene for me on subsequent occasions. Those repetitions effectively relieved all my feelings of guilt—and of sympathy, too.

Mrs. Gordon also replayed the angry scene for me—many times. Indeed, so many times did she replay it, often with Jeanie as the butt, that I got used to it. Ironically, I came to prefer her angry, and occasionally sad, moods to her very rare glad moods.

I don't know how I would feel about a glad Mrs. Gordon today. At age ten, I found her nauseating. Her face would be wreathed in forced smiles and her chatter was cloyingly sweet. On these occasions of gladness (mercifully rare), she would meet us at the door and seat us at the dining room table, which had been set with two napkins, a pitcher of milk, two glasses, two luncheon plates, and a serving dish heaped with Oreo cookies. Then, with too many smiles and winks and in a voice that could best be described as mealy, she would proceed to ask both her daughter and me (primarily me) questions about school. "Do you like your teacher? What is your favorite subject?" And always, "What did you learn in school today?" What bothered me especially was that her questions never varied.

I was part of this scene about a half dozen times. The first time only embarrassed me. After that, it angered me so much that I was tempted to change my answers each time. I had learned very quickly that what I said did not matter, as she never heard my reply anyway. I never did give in to my temptation because it would have embarrassed Jeanie far more than her mother annoyed me.

In May, about a month before the end of the school year, Jeanie moved to the north side of the city. Her move didn't concern me much, probably because eight-year-olds realize that they have little control over their lives, and even less over their environment.

The next time I saw Jeanie was when we were in high school. Curiously, we were both uncomfortable whenever we passed in the corridors, we would offer sheepish grins or nod faint "Hi's." To this day, I don't know why I never thought to ask her for a date.

Not until our 15th high school reunion did I talk to her again. She was drinking in the bar, alone.

Jeanie had never married. I don't know why, but I knew that the 15 years had not been especially kind to her. In high school, she had been a bit overweight. Now, at 33, she was just plain fat, and reminded me of her mother.

I said a warm hello, and asked about her mother.

She gave me a distant, indifferent look. Her answer was staccato-like, her words clipped. "She died last year. Cancer."

I was genuinely sorry, and told her that my own mother had also died of cancer.

She glanced at me sideways. Then the right corner of her mouth curled and jerked. Her reply, still staccato, came out mixed with spit. "Your mother had leukemia. A lot of people around her. Big funeral." In typical Joe Perez fashion, I had not remembered that she had been there. "Mine died of cirrhosis of the liver. Lushes," she said bitterly, "die alone."

Almost 25 years have passed since that meeting. I never saw Jeanie again. She died alone in an alcoholism detoxification center several years ago. I have thought about our last encounter many times, about how she had become so much like her mother. Somehow she had made me feel at fault, as if I had emotionally short-changed her, and her mother too.

More important, and more to the point here, I had not realized until Jeanie told me that Mrs. Gordon had been an alcoholic. I did not know it then, but Jeanie's final words to me, ironically delivered in a bar and badly mumbled, were to become impressed indelibly on my memory. In time, her phrase—"Lushes die alone"—came to serve as the catalyst that precipitated my thoughts about writing this book. In those words are both the theme and the rationale for this effort.

I am not sure how the Jeanie who died would have felt about the ultimate effects of her words. I know that the eight-year-old Jeanie would have been grateful.

I N T R O D U C T I O N

Introduction

Y ou may be alcoholic, have been reared in an alcoholic family, or
be married to an alcoholic. If your situation is one or more of these,
this book was written for you.

Among its worst effects, alcoholism has crippled your ability to
become involved in rewarding relationships. If touched by alcoholism
in your early years, you probably never learned how to develop such
relationships. Or again, you may find that you are unable to maintain promising ones—particularly with people of the opposite sex. In
short, you do not know how to get close, or how to stay close, to
people. People are a mystery to you, and if you are typical, you are
bewildered by the whys of all this.

This book will explain these whys through true stories, the stories
of men and women whom I have treated in psychotherapy. In one
or more of these stories, you will doubtlessly meet people you know;
indeed, you may even feel that somehow I learned of your story and
included it here.

The stories presented all concern unique and particular people.
And yet you will find that they all incorporate certain common
denominators in their personalities. These common denominators
stem from the fact that all of the people discussed in this book have
come into contact with alcoholism. The point? This insidious disease
affects all human beings in remarkably similar ways. Alcoholism
distorts one's perceptions of others, makes normal needs abnormal,
and erases conscience, and then often balloons it. Such effects invariably alienate the person from others.

This book was written also for those of you who *relate* to people
emotionally crippled by alcoholism. Through the stories and their
subsequent interpretations, you will gain new insights into the per-

sonalities of those who are alcoholically diseased. These insights concern such traits as why affected individuals are submissive, why they
are controlling, why they avoid honest communication, why they are
so unhappy with themselves, why they need constant approval, why
they cannot persevere with a task, why they are terrified of being
evaluated, and why their lives are so frantic—and on and on. In sum,
what I treat here are the dynamics that ultimately can destroy your
relationships with these victims of alcoholism.

The information in this book will do more than foster understanding; it will provide you with the rationale to *not* behave in ways that
feed their neurotic behavior. More important, these insights, together
with the specific lists of *do behaviors*, will equip you to behave in
ways that can ameliorate, if not alleviate, the insidious effects of
alcoholism in your relationship.

1

M A R T H A

"I Just Want to Die!"

"I just want to die. I just want to die." The young woman screamed, slurring the words. Her arms were slashing the air, her face a shade past vermillion, as she was wheeled in on a stretcher. This is my first recollection of Martha.

Twenty-four hours later, she was sitting, or, more accurately, sprawling, on a recliner chair in my office. She looked as she was supposed to look the day after her first admission to an alcoholism detoxification center—depressed.

I greeted her with a little smile. "Rough, eh?"

Her reply came back in a flat, hollow tone. "The pits."

While she stared stonily past me out the window, I glanced again at her admissions forms, which were virtually blank. In fact, the only items noted were her last name, Watson, and her address, a side street on the west side of town. The west side contains old, stately, very expensive homes.

I looked up, waited for her to break the silence, but doubted she would. Her facial expression and body posture literally and effectively reiterated her screams of last night, "I want to die!"

I looked at her. Five feet four, or five inches tall, weighing about 115 pounds. Her hair, cut short, was a mass of black tight ringlets, and contrasted startlingly with her complexion, which was so white that it reminded me of alabaster. The wide mouth did not jibe with the pug nose. Still, she struck me as very pretty.

3

I broke the silence. "You live on Victoria Road?"

"Yeah."

"Alone?"

She turned dark eyes on me. "No. With my parents. I'm 26 and still living with my parents. Pretty much sums me up, uh?"

I shook my head. "Nobody can be summed up in one fact." The conviction in my voice told her that I believed what I was saying. Still, she shrugged and gave me the cynical, disbelieving smile of the alcoholic.

Time passed, almost five minutes.

Again I broke the silence. "You're feeling real down on yourself." When I am still trying to develop rapport, I have an unfortunate penchant for stating the obvious. Sometimes it backfires (clients can become cold or hostile). This time there was no backfire. Martha gave me a smile, a genuine one. The words, however, were tinged with irony. "You have to be a doctor to figure that out, huh?"

I shook my head. "Just a person. How can I help, Martha?"

"Nobody can help."

I had heard that line before, dozens of times. It is a common one in the repertoire of the alcoholic with a hangover. What I have learned is that a sense of hopelessness and hangovers go together.

"Not much point in going on, eh?" My tone was facetious.

Her response was not. "I want to die."

I had discounted those words, delivered in wails and screams, the night before. I did not now. The blend of conviction and despair in her tone made me realize that this was not the idle talk of one hung over. Martha really did want to die! Suddenly an unwanted feeling, inexplicable and eerie came over me. It told me that Martha was going to carry out her wish.

"Why don't you tell me about it?"

"About what?"

"Your being here."

"What's to tell? I'm a drunk and a bore."

I shook my head. "Drunks are interesting." (I meant that.)

She ignored my comment, and continued to look at me stonily.

"Why are you a drunk, Martha?"

She shrugged. "I don't know and I don't really care why. I am. I just am. That's the reality."

"And you don't have any control over that?"

Her reply came back, flat, detached. "No."

That 'no' reflected the perception of a hard-core alcoholic. It told me that Martha perceived an indifferent, if not cruel, world filled with people who either did not care at all, or were bent on manipulating her for their own ends. In either case, as Martha saw it, she was a victim.

Several minutes passed. Then I noticed that Martha's eyes had brimmed up. I handed her a tissue. She wiped her eyes and began talking.

"My father's a lawyer—very busy, very successful. My mother is a frau, a boring hausfrau." Her description of her mother was framed in heavy sarcasm.

"You don't think much of your mother?"

Her tears stopped. Her voice again took on an indifferent tone. "Hard to think much about a nothing."

"So," I said, too briskly. "Daddy's a successful lawyer. Mother's a housewife and a nothing."

She nodded. "Never could figure out why they got married. They're so different. He's alive and energetic. She's in a constant state of tired. When I was a kid, he got me my breakfast and took me places. She slept."

Martha looked up. The tears had surfaced again. "She's alcoholic."

"Was she while you were growing up?"

"Ever since I can remember. And I've become just like her—boring, alcoholic, and a nothing!"

I shook my head. "Martha, you're not your mother."

Martha gave me a soft, ironic look, then shook her head slowly. "I don't want to become like her and live the nothing life she has but I see myself doing exactly that. That scares me, and what scares me even more is that little as she is, and she is a real nothing, she's still more, a lot more, than I am or will be."

"Why?" I asked curiously.

"When she was 26, she had been married for three years. I was already a toddler. Me, I'm still looking. Looking," she said with positive verve, "but not finding."

I wanted to respond with positive, soothing, and realistic words, like, "You're not your mother. You're a different person, brought up in different times." Instead, I said nothing. The alcoholic revelling alternately between self-pity and self-flagellation is not interested in reassurance.

She continued. "Do you know, I'm a college graduate and I don't have a job?" She smirked. "Jobs are like guys for me. They last about three months." She looked away. "You're right. I'm not my mother. But I'm not a different person. I'm like her—lazy, alcoholic, and boring."

"Why do you keep referring to yourself as boring?" I asked that with a hint of irritation in my voice. "You're articulate. Articulate people are not boring."

"My mother's articulate and she's boring. She's got about as much personality as a lukewarm cup of weak tea."

Despite my chuckle at her quip, I was worried. I began to understand a little of the why for my eerie feeling. Martha harbored incredible hostility toward her mother; although she did not respect her at all, at the same time she very much identified with her! Such dynamics, unfortunate indeed, are not uncommon in families. When you add alcoholism to these dynamics, however, the stage has been set for tragedy.

I told her that I had been in the emergency admitting room when she came in. "Did anyone accompany you or were you alone?"

Her answer, both in tone and content, was classically alcoholic. "I'm always alone."

I responded in a deliberately impatient tone. "Let's skip the bullshit, O.K.? We both know that if you're alone, it's because you choose to be."

Her head jerked up. She gave me a little bewildered smile. Candor confuses alcoholics—probably because they harbor it so little, see it so rarely. She nodded, spoke in a small voice. "I was alone. No one came with me. It's February. My parents are in Florida."

"You admitted yourself?"

"No. Mark had me admitted."

"Mark?"

"The last in my long line of lover boys. He came to the house. Let me make love to him."

Her phrasing puzzled me. "He let *you* make love to *him*?"

Her eyes leveled into mine. She spoke matter of factly. "Oral sex. I'm good at it."

I think my eyes betrayed a smile. Whatever Martha's problems might be, discussing preferred sexual techniques was not among them.

She nodded. "He got his jollies off, then gave me the happy news that we had to cool it."

"Why?"

"His wife suspects."

"Did you know he was married?"

She shook her head. "When he told me, I guess I went a little crazy. I chug-a-lugged about a quart of vodka. He called the ambulance and left me." She looked at me with a sad, childlike expression. "I'm a loser. Always seem to end up with a man who can't, or won't, marry me."

"There have been other married men?"

She nodded. "Four or five. Either they were divorced and afraid to remarry or they were guys who claimed they weren't the marrying kind. Always something. Anyway I always end up with nothing. Every affair, and that's all it ever is, starts off real torrid and ends up in a fizzle."

Our first session ended there.

Reflections

My first impressions are that Martha's alcoholism, a complement to or the result of her depression, is a function of her conflict between being identified with her mother and perceiving her mother as a "nothing." To see her mother as a nothing explains why she sees herself as a nothing. The conflict is heightened, the pain made more acute, by the fact that she sees her father as competent, powerful, and a person of considerable status. This is probably how she perceives men. I suspect, but don't know for sure at this point, that she is alternately fascinated and bewildered by them. She may also be scared of them. There is little doubt that she structures her relationships with them to fail. The why of that lies in her very confused perception of them. To understand the why of that confusion I needed to have more information about each parent and about their relationship.

POSTSCRIPT

I realize that I must keep in the forefront of my awareness that these are not conclusions but "tentative awarenesses." This is especially true regarding Martha's "basic" identity conflict.

At our second session, my general first impressions were confirmed. To my question, "Why do you think you're attracted to married men?" she responded sullenly, "I'm not attracted to married men."

"You're not attracted to them?"

"No."

I sighed. I hate to duel with and ultimately corner a client, especially an alcoholic. I have to. And I have to because alcoholics stay alcoholic precisely because their perception of self, and consequently their relationships, is distorted by denials that could best be termed bizarre, if not psychotic. Those denials must be confronted if they are going to make changes in their self-destructive life-styles. With a gentle tone, I posed my question. "Why do you date them?"

Martha sighed. "I don't know why." The perplexity with which she answered was real. After a long pause, she said, "Maybe it's because I can't find any guys who are single. When you're 26, the men are either too young or married."

I repeated her words, my tone flat. "They're either too young or married."

"Yes!" she said loudly.

"You don't have any choices." I had intended to keep my tone flat and was surprised by the edge with which my words came out.

She picked up on it. Eyes blazing, her reply came back sharp and shrill. "You're right. I don't have any choices, and don't make fun of me."

I shook my head. "I'm not making fun of you."

"I don't need your sarcasm then."

"None intended." I chuckled.

"Well, what are you trying to do? Why are you badgering me?"

I answered her simply and honestly, "I want to help you understand why you set yourself up to fail."

Her brows raised. She seemed startled. "With men?"

I nodded. "With men. With people. With life."

She looked at me squarely. "I'd give anything to be able to do that."

"I'm sure. Let's try again. Why married men?"

"You ask the question like you know the answer."

Alcoholics, when not under the influence of their drug, are exquisitely sensitive to the most hidden feelings and tones. Indeed, when sober, their emotional antennae miss nothing. This is why they are able to perceive the reasons behind another's words and veiled motives with disturbing accuracy. I confirmed her suspicion.

"I think you date married men because it's safe."

She laughed. "Safe how? Less likelihood of AIDS?"

I shook my head. "With a married man you don't have to get close, you don't have to worry about marriage."

Her surprise was genuine. "But I want to get married!"

I waited to respond, hoping she would get my point. She didn't. "If that's true, why do you date married men?"

Her mouth opened to respond, closed again. She looked away. "I told you why."

"All bullshit." I said lightly.

"It's not bullshit!"

I held my gaze, let a smile play around my mouth.

"You know, Doctor," she said through clenched teeth, "you can be infuriating."

I dropped the smile. "I know. With a married man you can comfortably delude yourself that you have a relationship and at the same time know in your heart that it will not be a meaningful one, one where commitments will have to be made."

Martha smirked. "Nice little analysis. The only trouble with it is that I don't know at the start that they are married. Only once did I know that. All the other times I didn't know it until it was over."

"Martha," I said, my voice deliberately heavy, "you knew it once and you continued in it. Right?"

She nodded.

"I'll bet all the other times you knew it in your heart."

"What's that mean? What's with this 'heart' talk?" The tone was sneering, but curious too.

"You knew unconsciously that they were married."

"Now *that's* bullshit!"

The utter conviction with which she yelled that shook me for a second, but only a second. I held her sudden, newly found hard gaze, repeated my impression, and added, "You gravitate toward married men. And the pull is almost like that, gravitational. You can't seem to help yourself."

My comments, at this point still more intuitive than reasoned out, were serving their purpose. They were precipitating a lot of feelings, albeit hostile ones. Always dangerous to a therapeutic relationship, hostility is still preferable to indifference—especially in an alcoholic, and particularly in a potentially suicidal alcoholic.

The feelings I was engendering in her showed on her face. Her inordinately pale complexion had developed a pink glow and her dark eyes were angry.

I spoke lightly. "I'm sorry if I made you mad."

"You're not," she spat. "You seem to be getting some kind of satanic pleasure from it."

She was right. I was pleased, but not maliciously. People who show their anger do not commit suicide. I smiled, "Right now you want to kill me."

"You're right!"

I nodded. "Good. That's healthier than wanting to kill yourself."

Her head jerked back. She smiled wryly. "That's debatable. World would miss you a lot more than me."

"Nobody loves you," I chirped.

"Nobody."

"Not even your parents."

"Especially my parents."

I leaned back in my chair. "Tell me, Martha, how do they get along?"

She shrugged. "Who knows?"

"Martha," I said with some impatience, "You live with them, and have, I guess, all your life. You must have some idea about . . ."

She interrupted. "We have an agreement, my parents and I. I don't know about them and they don't know about me."

"What does that mean?"

"Just that."

"You're telling me that you're emotionally divorced from them."

She gave me an ironic grin. "See how smart you are!"

"You're also telling me that you see them as allied against you."

"They're set up against me, yes. But they're not really allies. Allies are equal. They're not equals. Daddy's in charge."

"In charge of what?"

"Of her. Of him. Of them. He leads and she follows."

"You said that your mother was alcoholic?"

Martha's lip curled. "Yeah, she's that."

"How does your father feel about that?"

Martha looked away, shook her head. "I don't think he knows it, or at least he won't admit it. Mother hides it pretty well, and that's not hard because he's not home much. He leads a very predictable life. She knows when he's going to be home. So he never finds her really drunk, just a little high maybe. I've found her drunk now and then, and that's because I'm not predictable in my comings and goings."

"Has she found you drunk?"

"Yeah, they both have, but they don't, or won't, see me as alcoholic—my father especially. He thinks it's funny. He laughs about it, at least the last couple of times he did. He tells me that I'm cute when I've had a few." Again she looked away, and in a voice that made me think of tears, said, "We're a sick family. Sometimes I think my father, who seems to be the healthy one, is the sickest."

"Why do you say that?"

"He doesn't see my mother or me for what we are. He refuses to. Denial is supposed to be the defense on which alcoholism rests, at least that's what AA tells us, but my father, who isn't alcoholic, is the denier supreme."

"Yesterday you told me that he was competent, successful, energetic, and alive. You said all kinds of nice things about him. Today you tell me that he's sicker than you or your mother."

Her voice still tearful, she continued, "He's a competent lawyer but a failure as a father, as a husband, and as a human being."

I burrowed more deeply into my recliner as I held her gaze. Finally she was telling and sharing, something she needed to do if the therapy was going to have any meaning or value for her.

"How is he a failure?"

"He needs my mother and me to be sick."

"Why do you suppose that is?"

"Easy. He needs to be in control. Like most of you men, he's on a big power trip, has been all his life. He specializes in defending women who have been discriminated against. All crap. Truth is that my father is the biggest sexist and chauvinist going. He really believes women are lesser beings. 'Kinder, kirche, kuchen'—children, church, and kitchen. I read recently that that was the credo of the Nazis. It's my father's too."

"Does he abuse you or your mother physically?"

She seemed surprised at the question. "God no. Sometimes I almost wish he did. Horrible as that might be, it would show at least that he was emotionally involved. My father's abuse is more subtle. Did you know that you can be sophisticated in how you abuse people?" She nodded as she spoke. "Yes, you can. Benjamin Martin Watson is the living proof of that, of the sophisticated abuser. He never hits or slaps or even raises his voice." Her own voice had suddenly risen considerably. "He just quotes reasons. 'Let's reason together' is his favorite line with me. To reason together means to sit and listen to all the reasons why I should do what he wants. When I was a child, he used to 'reason' with my mother but now she never has to be 'reasoned with,' mostly because she now agrees with what he says or wants before he opens his mouth." She shook her head. "I swear, she's become a female clone."

"So what you're saying is that your mother anticipates his wants, has helped create a relationship that puts him in total control and that makes him feel like he's always in the right?"

Martha nodded and snickered, "He's always right. Anyway, when he comes on with that 'Let's reason together' bit I always feel like I'm stupid, unreasonable, or perverted if I don't agree, and do or say what he wants. And when he's doing this to me, she just sits there and plays his 'little Miss Echo'."

"How often does this happen?"

"Not too often anymore, mostly because I've learned to avoid them. I don't see them much."

"You don't eat together?"

"God no! They go out to eat a lot, mostly because my mother can't cook."

"Your life is a life alone," I observed.

She nodded. "Except for my boyfriends."

"No women friends."

She shook her head hard. "Not even one."

"Do you miss having them?"

She shrugged. "Like they say, can't miss what you never had." The thought was voiced in a way that made me think of a sad, acutely lonely little girl.

"Martha, have you thought about moving out?"

"All the time. What am I going to live on?"

"What do you live on now?"

"I work for a typing agency when there's work and I feel I need the money."

I nodded. I had the picture now.

"How would you feel about having your parents meet with us?"

"Why?"

"Why? Because you live with them, and frankly, if you're going to make any changes toward health, they're going to have to become involved."

She shrugged. "I told you that they are in Florida."

"Let's call them and get them up here. Can you do that?"

She shrugged. A surly expression had come across her face. "I'll see."

Our session ended.

Reflections

In reviewing the tape, I find that despite her attempt at suicide, Martha continues to harbor considerable strengths. These lie in her still strong curiousity to know about herself, and in her emotional repertoire. She can still get angry and can still indulge in ironic humor.

Of greater importance is her awareness of, even sensitivity to, the use of denial. Unlike most affected with alcoholism, Martha is very much aware of it in those closest to her, and even in herself. Thus, even though she steadfastly denied that she was attracted to men, she was curious to know my interpretation of it.

"Why married men?" I had asked and she had answered, "You ask the question like you know the answer."

Such a response reflected more than a latent interest in what I thought and indicates a receptivity to learning about herself and to moving toward health. Such interest and receptivity are the best antidotes I know to wanting to commit suicide.

At this point, I see the relationship with her father as a prime cause for her depression. The love/hate conflict with him is intense indeed. Freud would have had a field day with this case. The series of promiscuous and "safe" affairs with married men, he would say, can best be understood as unconscious, deep-seated attempts to seduce and get from daddy the love and attention she feels she never received. That they are married may also reflect something about how she perceives her mother—as a kind of nonstatus entity with whom she can effectively compete.

The lack of relationships with other women is not surprising. Indeed it is perfectly consistent, for it is symbolic of her lack of relationship with her mother. Sad but true, her mother has given her little or nothing emotionally or socially, and through her relationship with her husband taught Martha that women are zeroes. This is probably why Martha is not attracted to women. I suspect she perceives women with revulsion, which, of course, is how she perceives herself.

These parents have created a relationship and a home environment that have been singularly destructive for Martha. The perception of an uncaring, unloving, indeed cruel and threatening, world was acquired in this home environment. To return to it can bode tragedy. Yet this seems the way toward which she is bound.

Her response to my question, "Have you thought of moving out?" indicates that she feels she has no choice. "What am I going to live on?" was her reply. At the same time, she indicated that she worked only when the spirit moved her (or perhaps when she preferred not to ask daddy for money). Such a perception of her circumstances is in part created by herself, a victim's view. It is classically alcoholic. Combined with her lackadaisical attitude toward self-support, this view can only lay the basis for disaster.

The only alternative seems to be to help restructure the emotional climate at home. This is why I need to see the parents. It will be interesting to see if they are willing to return from Florida.

POSTSCRIPT

It was only when I was driving home that I realized the why of Martha's sudden surliness at the close of the session. In telling her (I thought I did it in a nice way) to call her parents, I had inadvertently, stupidly, stepped into a daddy role, and had thereby engendered a kind of little girl reaction.

That evening I received a call from Florida. Calls from patients' relatives, parents especially, are usually laden with anxiety. Not uncommonly, I have to suffer a lot of hyperbabble, a lot of disjointed, irrelevant questions, occasionally abuse. There was none of that from Frances Watson. Her message was short: her tone, cool and sophisticated, communicating her concern, as did her words. "We'll be flying home tomorrow morning early." We made an appointment for early afternoon. I hung up thinking that she did not fit Martha's description of a nothing person.

Martha and I were chatting when Benjamin and Frances arrived. Martha didn't get up, but gave them a kind of shame-faced greeting. Benjamin shook my hand, and going over to Martha, patted her head, and pecked her on the forehead. Frances gave her a little hug and a bright smile, and sat down on the two-seated couch opposite Martha and me. Benjamin sat next to Frances.

They didn't look as I had pictured them; both appeared much younger than they had to be. Benjamin was a little over six feet tall, slim, and with a full head of sandy hair. Frances could have passed for Martha's older sister, and not a much older one at that. The resemblance was striking in face, build, and hair. Frances wore more makeup than her daughter and exuded a strong but not unpleasant aroma of perfume.

Both looked remarkably composed considering the fact they had spent the day flying and in airports. They were dressed casually but expensively—she in a plaid wool skirt and red sweater, and he in brown slacks and a camel hair jacket that coordinated perfectly with the tan stripe in the blue mock turtle-neck shirt.

Benjamin leaned back in the couch.

Frances leaned forward, riveted black eyes on me, spoke quietly, "Fill us in, Doctor."

Martha answered before I could. "I can do it, Mother."

Her mother glanced at her and raised her right eyebrow, communicating condescension.

Martha ignored the look, and speaking rapidly, summarized the events since her admission. Both parents kept their eyes on me while she spoke. Frances maintained an impassive expression, Benjamin nodded, and smiled benevolently as if his daughter were making a flawless classroom recitation. She finished with "Well, what have you got to say?"

Frances' impassivity evaporated. She turned to her daughter and spoke coldly and in a voice that told us all that she was having trouble controlling her anger. "What do you expect us to say? That we're pleased? We're pleased that our 26-year-old daughter is admitted to a hospital like a common drunk? Dear God, child, how could you!"

I half expected her to add, "what will people think?" Her anger didn't surprise me. In fact, it gave me a sense of relief. It was normal, healthy even, and showed caring, even if in a less than desirable way. Her use of the world "child," however, did take me by surprise. While it jibed with her condescending look of a moment before, it struck me as unnecessary, if not cruel.

Martha must have felt the same way because she jumped up and screamed, "I'm not a child."

Benjamin gave the ceiling a weary, patient look, then seemingly pleased to be a mediator, nodded from one to the other. "Ladies, ladies."

Martha sat down. "I'm not a child!" She repeated this with the same verve but at half the decibel level.

Benjamin nodded in agreement. "Of course you're not. You just went and overdid it. Big deal. No one was really hurt by it." He said that in a soft, reassuring voice.

Martha shook her head, "You don't understand, daddy. Neither of you understands."

Frances glared. "When you speak in that patronizing voice I could cheerfully slap you."

Martha returned the look. "Guess where I learned it."

Benjamin gave the ceiling another look, then winked at me as if to say, "See what I have to put up with?" He spoke. "With all this silly squabbling," he said, "you haven't had a chance to say much."

I grinned, "I'm learning a lot."

A look I interpreted as scared flitted across his face. "What are you learning?"

"There's a lot of bewilderment, hostility, and confusion in the family, but not much communication."

Benjamin leaned back as if he were perfectly comfortable with my remark, then folded his arms barrierlike across his chest. "Tell us what you mean," he said in a voice that continued to ooze agreeability.

"Mr. Watson," I said evenly, "your family is an alcoholic family."

Benjamin must have prepared himself for my comment. His facial expression did not change, his arms remained folded. He just looked at me. I found the pause uncomfortable.

Frances broke it. "What are you saying?" she asked nervously.

Benjamin dropped his arms, leaned forward, and repeated his wife's question in a voice that matched the anger that suddenly appeared on his face.

"What he's saying, daddy," drawled Martha, "is that I'm an alcoholic. I told him that mother is one too!"

Benjamin turned to her slowly, and in a tone that could best be described as vicious spat out, "I asked him, not you."

I cleared my throat. "What I'm saying, Mr. Watson, is that Martha is indeed alcoholic. The simple truth is that when one member of a family is alcoholic, every member is affected."

"I'm not," he said brightly.

I ignored his remark and turned to Frances. "Martha tells me you have a drinking problem."

Like Martha earlier, Frances jumped up. "That's a despicable lie and she knows it," she cried, pointing but not looking at Martha. "There was a time when I may have drunk a little more than I needed to but I haven't had a drink in several years."

"Doctor, my wife and I flew up from Florida to be here with Martha in her time of trouble. We came to help. We didn't come to be insulted."

"Mr. Watson," I said quietly, "I'm not interested in insulting either you or Frances. I *am* interested in helping you understand that Martha is alcoholic."

"Who says so?" Benjamin asked in a tone so belligerent that I felt my stomach spasm in fear.

"I say so, daddy," said Martha in a small voice. All the anger she had expressed during the past couple of days no longer was in evidence.

"All right," said Benjamin in a voice suddenly expansive, "I like to think I listen. I like to think I'm reasonable. If you're convinced you're alcoholic, we'll send you to the best retreat whatever the cost, to dry out, recover, or whatever they do in those places out in the boondocks."

"Mr. Watson, you should know that in those places they recommend, often require, involvement by family members, and especially parents if children are going to be treated."

Benjamin nodded. "Whatever we need to do to help."

"Mr. Watson," I said, "my sense right now is that you have effectively divorced yourself from Martha's alcoholism."

"But I haven't," he cried. "I just told you I'll pay for the best treatment and I'll cooperate with whatever they ask." He looked at his wife. "We both will. Right, Fran?"

"Of course." Frances smiled at her daughter.

I looked from one to the other, gave another try. "The current thinking in alcoholism counseling is that every member of the family is part of the drinking member's problem."

Benjamin's eyes narrowed. He spoke in a way I had not heard yet. His voice was tempered, dispassionate, and steel-like. It reminded me of a judge, very sure of himself, who was handing down an opinion on a controversial issue. "Thank you for telling me what the current thinking is. You should know Doctor, that I occasionally deal with psychologists in my practice, and what I've learned is that you people aren't all that sure about what you're doing. You follow every fad and fashion coming down the pike. This week the thinking is one way, next week it's the opposite. Well, my thinking is consistent, and it's based on what I see. Frankly, I haven't seen her drunk—a little tipsy once in a while, but alcoholic?" He shook his head. "Not that! But then again, I'm a reasonable man. If she says that she thinks she is, I'll agree with her. I like to think that she is the best judge of her own body and mind, although, to be honest with you, I have my doubts about that." The look he gave his daughter could have been that of a social worker looking at a client. "No offense, honey, but you've never seemed to be too sure about what you want."

Frances chimed in. "Amen."

"Anyway," continued Benjamin, "I don't for a minute buy what you're saying, that my wife and I are part of the problem. Pure and simple, the problem is her problem, not ours. I'll assume the financial responsibility if she wants to be cured. But I do not agree that we're responsible for making her alcoholic—if she is. If she is, she made herself that way. We stopped watching her and supervising her every minute about 20 years ago." He turned to his wife. "Got anything you want to add?"

She gave him a pleasant nod. "I think you said it all."

He had indeed said it all. He had left nothing out. I glanced at Martha. She was staring stonily at the wall. Her look and body set were the ones she had assumed in our first moments together when she was still suffering a hangover and the acute pangs of guilt for trying to kill herself by chug-a-lugging a quart of vodka. Benjamin's diatribe had told me I was shoveling seaweed against the tide. It had also reinforced everything Martha knew and felt about her parents.

"O.K., Doctor, what now?" he asked brightly.

"It's up to you, Martha." I reexplained the rules I had explained to Martha earlier. Detox admissions could be released as soon as they felt able, and had to be released after three days. Only for extraordinary reasons could they stay as long as five.

Martha shrugged. "It doesn't matter."

Benjamin promptly gave me an "I told you so look," then turned and spoke pleasantly to his daughter. "It does matter, Martha, because you're important."

He turned to me. "Do you think we ought to put her in a retreat? I meant what I said. She doesn't have medical insurance but it doesn't matter. We want to do what's best for her."

I looked at Martha. "It's up to you. If you want more time to decide, alone, with me, you can stay another day, two even, if you think it's necessary."

She shrugged.

Frances sighed in exasperation.

Benjamin spoke, in another voice I had not heard. It sounded like a purr. "Take the time you need, honey. Take the time you need with the doctor."

Martha didn't reply, just stared stonily.

Benjamin's soft purring continued. "If you feel you're alcoholic, then you probably ought to go into treatment. Admission to some kind of retreat probably would be the way to go, but it's your decision. Yours! It's whatever you want, and I want to stress that."

Martha looked down at her lap, spoke just above a whisper. "I know, daddy."

The session ended a few minutes later.

Reflections

An extraordinary session, dominated by Benjamin. In physique, dress, and grooming, he projected the image of a dynamic, competent, and effective man, who expects to be in control always. Supremely self-confident, he is quick to communicate the idea that he can and will solve any and all problems that might come his way.

Communication is Benjamin's forte. His words impact exceedingly well because they ride on a kaleidescope of emotions. Anger, agreeability, love, impatience, steel-like hardness, a purring softness, and vitriol are all integral parts of his emotional repertoire, and he uses them all to advantage. Watching Benjamin talk and react was like watching a kind of human chameleon in action. His agreeability dazzled, his purrs camouflaged.

Like the chameleon, Benjamin's system of communication is intended to confound perception. With the chameleon, it ends there. With Benjamin, it is the foundation for his manipulation of those with whom he interacts. When Benjamin purrs, it is to persuade. When he is agreeable, it is to effect agreeability. And if these techniques do not work, he sheds the chameleon approach, explodes with vitriolic anger, and intimidates.

In a previous session, Martha had described her mother as Benjamin's female clone. In this session, her mother appeared to be just that in the youthful image she projected through her dress and grooming. In other areas, I didn't see the clone so much as the "little Miss Echo" Martha had quipped about. Frances functions as her husband's affirmer, his witness to speaking truth. I can't conceive of Frances as ever saying no to anything Benjamin says or requests. Benjamin has pretty much taken over her life. Frances, if not happy with that fact, is apparently resigned to it. My surmise is that her alcoholism is the price she paid for it. In some measure, her alcoholism can be understood as a product of the surrender of her personhood. Her conflict, anxiety, and depression at being "taken over" probably facilitated her alcoholism. Once the takeover was complete, once cloned, her need to drink abated. On this topic of her alcoholism, her strong protests that she has not had a drink for some years indicated that if she does not now have a problem, she certainly did once.

Martha's alcoholism can also be understood as a symptom of her struggle not to let happen to her what happened to her mother. When Martha told me that she did not want to be like her mother, what she was saying was that she did not want to be her father's clone. Her terror is that ultimately she will become precisely that. She saw him work his magic on her mother. She had learned a long time ago that Benjamin gets what he wants. In Martha's view, his confidence portends success, and his energy guarantees it.

These realizations dishearten me much. I am not optimistic about the outcome of this case. The prognosis has to be poor because Benjamin has presented her only two alternatives: clonism or escape into an alcoholism he will conveniently deny until she has regressed into something less than a person. I fear for her.

Epilogue

I never was to see any of the Watsons again. However, within a week of her discharge, I received a letter from Martha, written from an alcoholism treatment center in northern Vermont. "And no, doctor, I wasn't roaring drunk when I was admitted. They claim they treat the whole person here, not just the alcoholism. That's why I chose this place. All of me needs to be treated. Please write. I could use a pen pal."

I wrote when I could, she almost daily. The letters were a great therapeutic medicine for her. She poured out her heart, revealed a scared, bewildered young woman who nevertheless harbored a strong, unbounding determination to get well. She always finished her letter with, "I'll make it, you'll see—you'll see—you'll see."

Her last letter from Vermont was short but happy, enthusiastic even. It told me that she was leaving the hospital and had found a job as a teacher's aide in our local school system. It also told me that she would be living in her parents' home "but only till I've saved enough money to put a month's advance on my own apartment."

Less than a month after that letter, she phoned to thank me for my letters and my general support. She was still at home but was leaving shortly. There was an evasiveness, an elusiveness, about her that made me feel queasy. More disturbing was the proper, cool quality of her voice. It just did not jibe with the candid young woman I had seen in therapy or with the Martha who had written emotionally forthright letters. When I hung up, I realized she had sounded just like her mother. Clonism, I concluded, had been preferable to alcoholism.

The next day the local newspaper carried her picture and less than 50 words about her on its obituary page.

Martha and I were not related. We were not even friends. Our relationship came from counseling. The counseling relationship, however, is unique. It is not like a relationship between parent and child. It is not like the relationship between siblings. And it is not a relationship between peers either. It is simply not a friendship!

Rigidly structured within a professional code, the counseling relationship is positively enigmatic in that it engenders all the warmth, all the love, of all human relationships. It does so precisely because it is an encounter between two beings whose job is to explore and confront the whole spectrum of emotion.

And so when I read that obituary, I wept.

2

A L I C E

"It's People Who Make People Grow."

first met Alice at a three-day alcoholism seminar that I was giving for first-level managers in the local plant of a major corporation. The 25 managers sat at long, wide tables set up in the shape of a horseshoe. I presented and led discussion from the space created between the ends of the horseshoe. Alice sat at the middle of the table from which the sides branched. In that seat, she had high visibility. But she would have had it in any case. The expression on her face guaranteed it. Right from the start she looked very unhappy. I could not tell if she was hostile or scared. Her pursed lips wrinkled the edges of her mouth and made her look angry. A watery film magnified the pain in her eyes. My first impression of Alice was that she was desperately try-ing to contain an oversupply of gas that was being generated in the passageway between stomach and bowels.

There was another reason Alice had high visibility. She is not tall, about five feet three or four, but she is fat. Very fat. Her stomach pro-trudes as far as, if not beyond, her very considerable bosom. Alice must weigh over 200 pounds.

Unlike the other participants during the first hour of our session, Alice took no notes and asked no questions. She sat stiffly, clutching her oversized pocketbook tightly against her bosom as though it were a security blanket, and in the process she created a symbolic, yet very real, emotional barrier between herself and the rest of us. Lips pursed, eyes watery, she fixed on me with a kind of catatonic stare.

I decided I had to get her involved. With a smile and a nod, I asked, "What would be a sure sign of a drinking problem among the people you manage?"

Neither stare nor posture changed. Her reply, through still pursed lips, came back in a drawl that matched the words perfectly. "I haven't the vaguest idea." Quite apparently the naked hostility of such a comment can only dampen group interest or interaction. My impulse was to respond in kind. "What the hell are you doing here?" Since such a reply could only have compounded problems both for the group and for me, I gave her another little smile and moved to another participant with my question.

At midmorning break, I watched her relate to several of her colleagues. Her talk was cordial, deferential even, and softly modulated. I could not help but notice that her one-on-one interactions with each of the three people was accompanied by the consumption of a cheese danish. Three people, three danish, and all in the space of 15 minutes! The eating fit her size but the nice, easy way she had with her friends did not jibe at all with her response to my question. It set me to thinking.

I stayed close to her in the lunch line, and then sat opposite her at a small, square, two-person table. Her cool, indifferent response to my conversation while we were eating reinforced my thoughts even more. My sense was to confront. I did it.

I put down my teaspoon, watched her fork down the last of her mashed potatoes. "Alice, you know about alcoholism."

Her head jerked back. "What do you mean?"

"Just that. You know about booze and what it can do."

She ate faster, didn't look at me.

"Let me know if you want to talk." I put my professional card on her tray.

Alice's demeanor changed during the afternoon session. And even though she didn't interact with comments or questions, her expression had softened. The hard rigid stare and the wrinkled angry look around her mouth were both gone.

At the end of the day's session, I found her waiting for me at the entrance to the plant. She greeted me shyly and walked with me to my car. "How did you know about me knowing about alcoholism?" she asked with embarrassment.

"I didn't know. I suspected. You were so nice to others at the break that I knew your coldness and hostility toward me were not personal because we don't know each other. It had to be the topic. And if it made you act like that, I figured you were afraid of it."

When we got to my car, she spoke in a low, confidential voice, as if afraid to be overheard. "You're right, and I'd like to take you up on your offer. I'd like to talk to you."

I smiled. "Good!" I told her to call my office for an appointment.

She started to hurry away, turned, "By the way, will my medical plan here cover it?"

I waved reassuringly as I climbed into my car. "Every penny."

Alice never came back to the seminar. She explained at our first counseling session that groups, small groups especially, made her feel very nervous and self-conscious. "I can only handle one person at a time," she said.

"So why did you sign up?"

"I thought it was going to be just informational. Nobody told me I had to participate."

"Group participation makes you nervous?"

"Yes."

"Any special reason you wanted to see me?"

Alice shifted and looked away. "No special reason, just that my life's a mess." She punctuated that with an uneasy laugh and began to talk.

After only a few minutes, I was inclined to agree, her life was a mess. She described her husband as an unemployed house painter who was away more than home. When around, he abused her physically. Her daughter, a 16-year-old, had quit school and run away from home and her 20-year-old son had fathered two children by two different teenage girls. "I learned about the second one the day I met you at the seminar." Throughout the first session there was a latent, but constant, victimlike whine in her voice, quite common in women who have lived with alcoholism.

She talked eagerly, almost happily, at a machine-gun-like pace, barely drawing a breath between sentences. I had no chance to reflect, respond, or comment. Alice, I learned quickly, was an acutely lonely woman who had had few, if any, opportunities to share the horror and trauma of a life of emotional deprivation.

She was the only child of an alcoholic mother. Her father had deserted the family before or right after she was born. She never knew him. She characterized her mother "as a woman with no skills, no education, and no energy." Her entire childhood had been spent in the same three-room, cold-water flat. They lived on city welfare and the charity of the local parish church, of which her mother was a nominal member. What she remembers is that while there were days without food, her mother always had a gallon of wine. "I remember as a little kid struggling with the big heavy jug, scared out of my wits that I'd spill wine or drop the bottle. I realize now that I put up with the awful fear because it was the only time she'd compliment me with, 'That's mama's good girl,' or something like that. Most of the time, especially when I was a little kid, she just ignored me.

"The only nice part of my childhood was school. I loved school, and I loved it because I was good in school. The teachers, all the teachers, liked me because I was smart. In the fourth and fifth grades, I was the smartest kid in the room. The teacher knew it. The kids knew it, and I knew it. Even though I had no friends, I never had any, I was looked up to, I had respect because I was smart. The fact that I was smart was probably the most important thing I learned in elementary school. My brains got me to go back to school, got me to go to college, got me through college, and got me my job. There's no substitute for brains. Don't let anybody tell you otherwise."

Alice ran out of breath for a second, permitting me to ask, "What did you mean when you said you went back to school? Did you quit?"

She nodded. Her watery eyes began to spill over. "I quit in junior high school. You know why I quit? I quit because I felt so weird, so different from the other kids. You know where my clothes came from? They came from a neighborhood thrift shop. You can imagine what a thrift shop in the poorest section of town has for clothes. Anyway, I felt weird and I looked weird."

She stopped talking for a moment. Tears streaming, she explained that these charity clothes were always clothes that were outmoded, and worse, were styled for children who were younger or older and never fit well. "I looked like what I was," she said bitterly, "an orphan. I stopped going to school when I was 13. Nobody missed me. I knew nobody missed me because I was more than 14 when the truant officer came to see me. He brought me the official dropout papers. I filled them out. I signed them. My mother never knew. That's how alcoholic she had become. I ran the house. I signed the welfare check. I did the shopping. I even bought her booze."

"At 14?"

She nodded. "At 14. Easy. I wrote a note and signed my mother's name. Liquor store owners want to sell booze. They don't care who they sell it to or who gets drunk on it."

She stopped talking, looked away, and gave a little tired sigh.

I leaned back. "Tell me, Alice, everything considered, what was the worst thing about growing up in your mother's house?"

She looked at me thoughtfully. "Lonely. I was alone all the time."

"Your mother wasn't home?"

"She was home. In fact, she never left the house. But I still was alone all the time. She never talked to me. She didn't seem to notice that I was home, unless she wanted me to go out for something. Ninety percent of the time that something came from the wine and beer store on the corner. All I had was a television set. Television was my companion, my teacher, the love of my life.

"I lived for the soap operas. They made my life worthwhile. Once the TV broke down. I walked from one repair shop to another asking to have a man come to repair it. When they heard our address, they would ask if we had the money to pay for it. When I told him we would have it at the end of the month, they said they would come then. Walking home that day from the fourth or fifth TV shop was one of the unhappiest times of my life. I was going to have to do without the only thing that mattered in my life. I never felt so lonely. I never felt so poor. I was so upset. I cried so that I walked past our house without knowing it."

Alice had started to cry, if possible, harder than before. Several minutes went by. Her body seemed to have gone limp. The catharses had taken their toll. She got up slowly, spoke hesitantly, "Doctor, I think I have to be going now."

I glanced at the clock. "But you still have almost 15 minutes, Alice."

Her tears had stopped. "I just think it would be better if I left now."

"Do you want to make another appointment?"

She didn't answer my question. "I'll be in touch. I promise."

Reflections

Apparently Alice has many personal problems. The most apparent symptom of those problems is her weight. In this world, where appearances are everything and a lean body is held in high esteem, I am sure she encounters condescension. Her response is to act with deference. Deference, especially one on one, is the response of the person who has low self-esteem. This same person does not like being the focal point of attention in a group. I believe her comment about being able to deal only with one person at a time.

Alice has been exposed to a life of deprivation and loneliness. Her life has brought her pain so acute that she cannot deal with it even after a quarter of a century.

Her initial enthusiasm to relieve some of that pain by sharing it with me wilted in about a half-hour. Has she become so used to living with this pain and the anxiety it engenders that she finds it preferable to letting it out? Perhaps. Emotional catharses can be devastating. To some individuals in pain, they are palpable proof that their troubles are even worse than they thought. My sense is that Alice will not return.

POSTSCRIPT

My sense proved to be only partially right. Alice was to come back to counseling, but not for a long time. However, within the week I received a letter from her, the first of many. A good portion of her story is told through edited letters.

"I never really thought about my life or talked about it with anybody until I was in your office. I guess I never did because it was painful. I didn't realize how terribly painful it was until I started to tell you about it, especially about when I was a little girl. I still think of myself as a little girl. I was pretty when I was in elementary and junior high school. I have pictures of me then, one a colored one. Yes, I was pretty. Today I'm big and fat and ugly.

"In my pretty days, nobody told me I was, certainly not my mother. I found out from the leers I got from older boys and men.

"I developed early. I was menstruating before I reached junior high. A big reason clothes never fit was that I grew so fast. I never went through any training bra stage like other girls. What I did go through was a long embarrassing period of bouncing and shaking, then into bras that were too small or too big. (Goodwill charities never had my size.) Anyway, there was a long period in my life when my body was a woman's but my mind, my experience, my know-how were those of a child.

"The kids my age giggled about my body. That embarrassed me. I began to hold my chest in and walk around like I was round shouldered. The so-called big boys didn't giggle. They leered. That scared me. But even though they made me nervous, I got all kinds of strange other feelings from their looks too. One of those feelings made me tingle all over. The one who made me tingle most was Jim. He lived in the apartment house next to ours. He had no father and lived alone with his mother.

"Jim was three years older than I and hung out on the corner with other boys. I tended to avoid that corner even before I began blossoming out. Groups of kids (boys especially) had always made me nervous. After the blossoming, my avoidance of that corner, and boys' groups in general, bordered on the phobic.

"Despite the phobia, I liked to watch them from the living room window. Jim, I noticed, was not as aggressive or as rambunctious as the rest of them. He didn't participate in their pushing, shoving, and horseplay. He stayed on the fringes of the group. I thought that he acted like me.

"I noticed that he always left the group at a little after 4 o'clock to be home for his mother, who came home from work at 4:30. I told myself that he was a good boy, and beautiful too—black curly hair, long, almost feminine eyelashes, and dark, dark eyes. Once when we passed on the hall stairs he had turned those eyes into mine. I oozed in my pants.

"I took to going downstairs just as I saw him leave his friends so I could be near the walk to his front door and mumble a shy 'hi' when he went in. It took me almost a week to observe that his 'hi' was said even more shyly than mine. The discovery gave me a real boost. It made me suddenly very confident. I started thinking up things to talk to him about. We never talked for more than a few minutes, but those minutes were enough to fulfill all my childish romantic fantasies. In no time I felt like the star in my own soap opera. Our few minutes of talk got longer and longer. Our shyness evaporated. He asked me out to a movie. We sat in the back and necked and petted and petted and petted . . . Within a few days of that date, Jim was not hanging out at the corner; he was in his house with me. We used his mother's big double bed. The mattress seemed high off the ground. It was the most comfortable bed I had ever lain in. Baby Jesus stared down from a picture, and I like to think blessed all the proceedings. Jim and I spent a lot of time on that bed.

"Usually girls like me in this situation are scared because of their ignorance and terrified that they're going to get pregnant. I wasn't in the least scared by either. In fact, I was amazed at how much I knew instinctively, and how much I enjoyed it.

"On the fourth of July, I figured out I was pregnant. Jim was in his kitchen making a peanut butter sandwich when I told him. His face screwed up all funny and the look he gave me made me want to die. All of a sudden, he slammed the cabinet shut, threw the knife, still covered with peanut butter, at the wall, and screamed, 'Jesus Christ almighty! How could you do that? Stupid! How could you be so stupid?' So ended my first love. I slammed out of his kitchen, stumbled downstairs to my house. I remember pacing back and forth for a long, long time from my small bedroom to the bathroom. I was confused, crying, and only dimly heard the familiar drunken snoring of my mother asleep on the living room couch.

"The worst feeling in the world is to know what you want but not know how to get it. I wanted an abortion. Naive as I was, I was smart enough to know that I didn't know anything at all about being a mother. Mine, I realized, was something less than an ideal model.

"The thought that buzzed through my head was that it wasn't just that I wanted one, I needed it. But I didn't have the foggiest notion of what to do, where to go, who to see about getting one.

"It had been almost three years since I'd been in school. I went back to junior high school. Walking back into that school was the scariest thing I ever went through. Looking back, it probably was the most courageous thing I ever did.

"Miss Jones was the guidance counselor. I told her that I wanted to come back to school. Then I started to cry. My tears were partly real, partly put on. Most of the real ones I had shed in my house.

"Miss Jones was smart. She knew right off why I was there. She was very nice and told me what I knew, that abortions were illegal. Then she asked me if I wanted her to arrange it. I nodded my head so hard she laughed.

"The next afternoon, right after school, she brought me to the neighborhood clinic, and in a little white room with her present, I had my abortion. She had prepared me by telling me what would happen. It was just like she said. There was no pain. The doctor shot something up my cervix and sucked out what was in there. It was over in a couple of minutes. All I remember about it is that the doctor had very pale skin and very hairy arms. I had no remorse then, and I don't now. I thank God I got rid of 'It' because I could never have given 'It' anything, not even love. That was what I needed too much myself.

"Yes, I thank God I had the abortion because by getting it, by asserting myself, I taught myself something that up to that point I had been unable or unwilling to recognize—I didn't have to be a victim. I had choices. *I* had chosen to get an abortion, and I had gotten it.

"The abortion did something else, something that changed my whole life. It led me back to school, and within three years I had graduated second in a class of 346. As second highest student, I had to give the class oration. The topic chosen by the principal was 'The Importance of Family Life.' I wrote it and delivered it. My mother wasn't there.

"A few of the teachers asked me where my mother was. I gave the answer I always gave on those rare occasions that anybody asked about her. She was sick with the flu. The truth was that I was glad she was not there. I would have been ashamed if she had come. Over the three years of my school career, she had deteriorated even more. She had become a recluse in every sense of the word. She never stepped outside of the house. She was drunk all the time, either in an awake kind of glassy-eyed stupor or dead to the world in a grunting-like snore that always made me think of an old sow.

"I did everything for her. She had regressed to the level of a baby. Weird but true. I had become my mother's mother. I signed and cashed the welfare check and handled all the finances, and even though I stretched every dollar like it was superelastic, I always ran out of money before the end of the month. Booze cost a lot even though I bought the cheapest I could find. To save still more, I watered it down by almost a third. Mother never seemed to notice. She never complained. She just drank it.

"My lack of clothes continued to be my major concern. Miss Jones, who was always dressed nicely, must have noticed how terrible mine looked and fit. One day she went to the neighborhood thrift shop with me to help pick them out. I sensed that she didn't think much of the place.

"The next day she told me about an after-school job in the local branch of the public library. It paid minimum wages but would provide me with the money to buy my clothes in a regular store.

"I took the job. It proved to be another turning point in my life. The work was less than easy. I was supposed to put books back on the shelf. Since reading was not the thing in our neighborhood, very few took books out and there was very little to do. I was so bored after the first day that I started to read. Up to that point, I had viewed reading as basically work.

"It was something I did to get my homework done. It was a school thing, an obligation, not especially hard, but not fun either. Fun was watching soaps. Anyway, I picked up a paperback from the shelf of romance novels, started reading, and *couldn't put it down*. My three work hours flew by. I took one home and finished it. By the end of the week, I'd read five or six more. My newly discovered interest quickly became a veritable passion. By the end of the month, I'd read every book on the shelf and was ordering ones we didn't have from the main library.

"The books were more than romantic stories for me. I lived them. Not only did I identify with the heroines, I became them, and found myself memorizing their lines. Every day I was another beautiful and fragile heroine, and if I suffered their cruel hurts, I was also transported by their ecstatic joys. (Every week I experienced a couple of wedding nights.) I began to live in a kind of blissful fantasy world while I waited for my Prince Charming to come charging up.

"On graduation night, the night I was star, my fantasy world turned real. My class oration started the program, put me in center stage. In my white dress with the wide navy-blue waist sash, I felt like my own heroine as I paraded back and forth for prizes, plaudits, and compliments.

"My sense of stardom was not just fantasy because after the ceremonies a group of kids I scarcely knew asked me to their party. Within minutes of stepping into the crowded, noisy kitchen, I had met him.

"At 19 he looked like Prince Charming was supposed to look—tall, blond, slim, and blue-eyed. Allen could have doubled for Robert Redford. He glanced down, flashed his broad, dimpled smile, and I melted, blushing under his wonderfully attentive gaze. He led me outside, sat me down on the porch stairs, and talked to me about me. His tone was soft and gentle as he told me how pretty I looked and how great my talk had been. 'Family is the whole thing,' he said in a slurred voice. I didn't notice the slurs, I just oozed my pants. He was so beautiful! Nobody that gorgeous had ever looked at me. On that blissful night I learned that daydreams and wishes can and do come true. We walked home like lovers do, his arm draped around my shoulders. Occasionally, he brushed my breast shyly, gently, and all the while he talked in a soft tone. By the time I got home, I was in that state of keen anticipation that all romantic heroines go through just before consummation of their love. We made ours in the soft ankle-high grass, in the backyard, under the stars. With Jim it had always been done too anxiously, too roughly, and too quickly to be romantic, or even pleasurable. Allen was tender, and despite our setting, relaxed, almost casual. But what convinced me that I'd found my man was that afterwards he hugged and held me like he meant it, and then he did what Jim would never have done—he thanked me.

"That night I slept the sleep of a woman fulfilled. Even my mother's snores sounded soft and gentle. They lulled me to sleep.

"Allen came around every day. The first time he showed up I was nervous because of the awful presence my mother made. In a drunken stupor, she shuffled into the kichen, poured vodka, and shuffled out. She never bathed herself. When her body odor got so that I couldn't stand it, I'd wait until she passed out (usually around eight o'clock) and I would undress her and give her a sponge bath. Then I'd dress her in clean clothes. The first time Allen came around, almost a week had passed since the last sponge bath. I knew she smelled.

"When she came in to pour her booze, Allen very discreetly didn't notice her. She came in a couple of more times during that first visit. I guess my embarrassment showed because I was walking him downstairs when he jerked his head toward our apartment door and said, 'My father's like her.'

"That information made me feel good. It made me feel like we had something important in common. We were both too naive, too young to know then that children can survive alcoholic parents only if they realize what an insidious curse they can be. I would come to understand that very, very slowly because of my anger. Allen never would.

"Allen spent most of the summer in my house, or more accurately, in my bedroom. From the first I thought that Allen's discretion and politeness with my mother were irrelevant because she never even noticed him. I was wrong. Once in her drunkeness she burst into the toilet when he was urinating. She mumbled an 'Excuse me,' edged out, and shot me a bleary look. 'You'd better watch out, child, that boy's hung like a Brahmin bull!' That was the first and the only comment my mother ever made to me that had to do with men or sex.

She wasn't to make many more of any kind because two months later, on a hot, sticky day in August, she died. I didn't know who else to call so I called the welfare office. A social worker made the funeral arrangements. Calling hours were the next day at a local funeral parlor. No one came.

"Sad but true, I did not mourn my mother's death. A decade of a zombielike indifference and neglect of me and herself had long ago erased any lingering feelings of affection. Her death was no more than an inconvenience because I had to fill out a lot of papers for the welfare people.

"The day after she died, Allen moved in. He was working as a house painter's assistant and earning over $200 a week in cash. He gave it to me to manage. By the middle of September, I had saved over $500. It was more money than I had ever had at one time. We bought a car, repainted the whole apartment, and got married."

Reflections

These letters tell the story of a child emotionally deprived of security and love. The constant message of this deprivation was that Alice was inadequate as a person. This sense of inadequacy in her development was compounded by a cruel poverty. The sense of inadequacy became so strong that she responded in the way she had learned from her mother—by isolating herself. It was precisely this self-imposed isolation that prevented her from learning about people and how to relate to them. Put simply, Alice never learned how to deal with real people in the real world. Her experience with Jim was the harshest confirmation of that fact. Reality, she learned from him, was nothing but a cruel ordeal. She distanced herself from it by steeping herself in a world of fantasy, first by her enchantment with television soap operas, then even more by her addiction to romance novels. Quickly, easily, the world of fantasy became her reality. My impression at this point is that it was with the emotional and interpersonal wherewithal of a very little girl that Alice married Allen.

Despite this background, this woman possesses considerable strengths. Her school achievements told her and us that she is intelligent and, more important, can solve problems. She herself interpreted her return to school as courageous. And well she might. Even more, her return to school reflected an energy, a determination "to make it" in a world that bewildered her and with which, through no fault of her own, she was so ill equipped to deal.

Finally, what these letters reveal is an articulate woman with an introspective bent. This last quality was undoubtedly the prime factor in her return to counseling.

Almost five months after the receipt of the last letter, Alice contacted me for an appointment.

The form-fitting blouse was striped, the skirt, burgundy colored, flared but very short. She whirled in front of me, "What do you think?" she asked brightly.

I didn't know what to think because I was having so much trouble believing that this was the same teary-eyed, depressed woman who had felt too fragile to cope with her own catharsis.

Alice looked great. Approximately four months had elapsed since our last appointment. She seemed to have lost 60 to 70 pounds ("74" she was to inform me proudly). I was more than curious to know what had precipitated the metamorphosis.

I looked and listened with all my emotional antennae, thinking that perhaps I was seeing a woman who was suffering from a mild hypermania. She wasn't. Her speech was steady, rational, and, more important, interesting. It contained none of the nonsensical irrelevancies common in maniacal talk.

Alice's new good looks were not limited to her new attractive figure. Her eyes, which had lost the teary film, had brightened, glowed even. In fact, all of Alice seemed to glow. She made me think of a woman in love.

I waved her to a recliner and settled into my own. "So," I said patting my own developing paunch, "how did you lose it?"

"Believe it or not, the letter writing helped. Helped a lot."

I believed. Having me to write to had provided her with an opportunity to look at herself and her life in a detached, intellectualized way without the emotionality invariably attendant in psychotherapy. "You look so good," I said, "life's got to be treating you better."

She smiled. "A lot of problems still."

"But you're coping."

"I'm coping, but I don't know how well."

I waited.

"It's my family."

"You told me about your 16-year-old daughter who ran away and your son who has fathered two kids with two girls."

"Jane's back home. She came back the last day I was here."

"How is it with the two of you?"

"Better. It's better."

"She never could have made it on the streets. She's too shy. Always has been. She came home and told me that she had run away because she couldn't stand watching Allen shit all over me. Those were her words, 'shit all over me.' She told me a lot of things. A lot. She told me she was ashamed of me, of how fat I was. She was so ashamed that she couldn't stand being seen with me. She cried while telling me that even more than I cried while listening to it."

"You cried because you realized that you had become just like your mother."

She nodded. "I cried for that, yes, but I cried more because I realized that Jane could become, would become, what I was, what my mother had been, if I didn't make some big changes—and fast."

It was all credible. I have learned that given the right circumstances, reasons, and motive, people can and do change their lives. "Just like that, you decided to make big changes?"

"Yes."

"What changes?"

"I filed for divorce and went on a diet. The judge granted the divorce. It will be final within four months." She leaned back, the satisfaction on her face transparent. "I got the divorce and the diet worked. I lost 74 pounds in a little over four months."

I uttered the words she wanted to hear. "You should be proud of yourself."

"I am," she said quietly. "I am proud of myself, and even though I feel a lot better about me, there are feelings I still have to resolve. That's why I'm here. And this time I'm not running away. I'm through running."

"What feelings do you need to resolve?"

"Guilt. I feel so damned guilty."

"About what?"

"About letting Allen shit on me for 20 years. And about Jane. Like me, she never had much of a mother. I've only now begun discussing anything meaningful like men and sex with her. I worry about her. I don't want her to be like me, naive and not knowing how to act with people, especially with boys. I worry about the fact that she never wants to go out with other kids. I worry, and I realize that she acts just like I did. As a teenager she's a carbon copy of me, of what I was. And I was not happy. God! How could I have done that to her!"

These last lines were punctuated with a distinct whine. The happy glow had left her face. The crystal-clear whites of her eyes had clouded over again. The guilt, not uncommonly, had blended with a strong element of self-pity, had effectively combined to erase the effervescence with which she had whirled in. I understand and tolerate guilt without much trouble. However, I have never been able to appreciate self-pity. I have learned that it is best to ignore it. To respond to it even with irony is to give it importance, or at least more weight than it merits. I addressed her guilt. "What you did to her is done. The past," I said in a heavily facetious tone, "is a canceled check."

"It isn't canceled for her. For her it's all too real."

"By real you mean horrible?"

"Worse than that. Allen's drinking was worse for her than my mother's ever was for me."

"Why?"

"She had to put up with his alcoholism and my craziness."

"Your craziness?"

"Yeah," she said looking away.

"Alice," I said, the hint of impatience deliberate, "Is there something you're not telling me?"

Still looking away she answered softly, "He abused her."

"Sexually?"

"Yes," she croaked.

Everything became instantly clear. "It's why she ran away?" I asked. "Yes."

"She blamed you for it?"

"Yes. Still does, I think."

Even though I knew, I asked, "Why?"

"She figures I knew that it was going on."

It still seems cruel to me when I do it, but I have to. The healing process cannot begin without the awful admission. I cleared my throat. My tone gentle, I posed the question, "And did you, Alice?"

Tears flowing, she nodded. "I knew. In my heart I knew, even though I wouldn't admit it in my head."

It was the classic alcoholic denial. "You're admitting it now. Have you admitted it to her?"

She nodded.

"And you've divorced him. That shows you're determined not to let him shit on you anymore. It shows you're strong, want to be your own person."

Then Alice screamed. "He screwed his own daughter and I didn't do anything about it!"

I sat quietly while she sobbed softly. I didn't talk because her dramatic scream had unnerved me momentarily.

"God," she moaned, "how could I have done that?"

"You feel a little like you were a party to it?"

"I was very much a party to it," she cried.

"Why do you say that?"

"I told you. I didn't do anything about it."

She was still revelling in self-pity. "Flagellating yourself just isn't going to help. It isn't going to do anything for you, or for Jane either. Denial is a powerful mechanism. People can discount even the most obvious reality if they feel it's too threatening or traumatic."

"I did that. I did exactly that. I denied everything that was happening. Jane told me that I was in the house sometimes when it happened."

"You were in the house." I repeat the client's words like that, in a flat, noncommittal tone, when I am at a loss.

"I was in the house," she repeated heavily. "Sleeping. Once I was in the living room watching a movie on TV. I denied it. She denied it."

"How do you know she denied it?"

"She told me. She goes to Al-Anon. That's where she learned about herself and Allen and me and the craziness she's lived with all her life. It was Al-Anon that sent her home to talk and cry with me."

"You told me she was denying it too."

"She was. That's why she and I talk all the time about everything. We've resolved not to deny anymore. My mother and Allen made me sick. It's sad," she said with a thoughtful look. "It's people who make people sick." Her face brightened, "But what I've learned from my daughter is that it's people who make people well."

"What you're saying, I think, is that if one member of the family is alcoholic, the whole family becomes alcoholic."

"Right. I never drank but I found I denied like an alcoholic. I guess I learned that from my mother. I denied everything—her acting like

a zombie, my loneliness, my naivite. I was and acted just like Allen.
It's probably why I married him. He acted in ways familiar to me
because he came from an alcoholic family too. I was comfortable with
him. He was with me. We found each other because in some kind
of crazy way we were comfortable with ways and cues and vibes that
were alcoholic." She shuddered. "Sick! And we made our beautiful
daughter sick. We made her so sick she began thinking that if it wasn't
perfectly normal for a father to fondle and have intercourse with his
daughter, then it wasn't so bad either. He told her that other people
did it. When she told me that, I realized that if she thought sex with
a parent is normal or O.K., then she could not possibly know what
normal was."

"And it was that realization that got you to move on the divorce."
"Yes."
"And in the process got you closer to your daughter."
"Yes."

Reflections

*Incest between father and daughter in an alcoholic family is not an
uncommon occurrence. Neither is a maternal denial of it. To some extent, Alice is still operating with that denial. The circuitous route she
took to tell me about it reflects not only the monumental guilt she still
feels but also indicates that she is still not comfortable with staying aware
of it, and especially with talking about it.*

*If anything, her strengths have increased. Painful as it is, she finally
is able to admit her denial of Allen's incestuous involvement. More important, while she is clearly able to admit to her responsibility, she is
very aware that she learned her denial from, and that her "craziness"
is a function of being sucked into, the alcoholic dynamics of, first, her
mother, and then Allen. Simply, she is aware that she learned her
craziness, and that her daughter did too. More important still, she is
equally aware that she can unlearn that craziness. "It's people who make
people well too." Finally and most significant, she looks well. Indeed, if
physical appearance is any criterion for evaluating emotional health,
we have to conclude that Alice's health has taken a quantum leap
forward.*

Alice spent the next session discussing Allen's alcoholism and its
effects on the family.

"As I recall from your letter, before marriage it was all good with him. He was caring, considerate, kind."

She nodded. "All of those things."

"What happened?"

"Booze," she said. "Booze happened. Actually, I'm convinced now that he was alcoholic when I met him. Like I told you before, we were both children of alcoholics. The alcoholism came out in both of us but in different ways, that's all. He turned out to be addicted to alcohol. Me, I became a mousey, doormat who made it easier for him to be alcoholic." With a shrug and more than a hint of irony she finished with, "I think the term is 'enabler.'"

"At what point did you realize that he was alcoholic? Early or late in your marriage?" These are important questions. The replies indicate to what extent the enabler fed into the process and became a part of it.

Alice shook her head. "I'm not sure. The other day while driving I had a thought that I shared with Jane, and I wanted to ask you about it."

"Ask."

"Do you think I got fat because Allen is alcoholic?"

"I don't know, but I'm curious. What made you think that?"

"I gained an awful lot of weight with Bobby, my first child, and never really lost it."

"So?"

"I think I was depressed all the years I was married. I think that very early in our marriage, even before Bobby was born, and he was born seven months after we were married, I felt like I'd gone from the frying pan into the fire. I was alone all the time. It was funny. My mother had never left the house but he was never in it. Either way, I was always alone. Started right after we got married. He didn't come home till late at night."

"And he was drunk?"

"Almost always. When he wasn't, he demanded sex. It was so different from when we were lovers. He put on a wedding band and became a drunken bastard. Like I told you in my letters, before we were married he always thanked me. After we were married, he'd just roll off me and snore off his drink.

"Once right after I had Bobby, Ms. Jones came to visit with a baby gift. As it happened, Allen was home. I introduced them. And you know what? I introduced him as my mother! Honest to God, I said that! I said, 'This is my mother' to Ms. Jones. She laughed. Allen got mad. I was so embarrassed, I blushed."

"So what you're telling me is that Allen had blended for you with your mother. What you saw and felt, but couldn't admit, was that Allen was just like your mother, alcoholic."

"Yeah."

"You felt like you had married your mother."

"Precisely."

"And you think that feeling got you so depressed you made yourself fat."

"What do you think?"

"It's possible."

"If nothing else, it would explain why after I divorced him I found it so easy to lose weight. And I did. Everybody I know is more impressed with my weight loss than I am because they all think it was so hard. It was easy."

"And it was easy because there's no longer any need to be depressed."

"Yes."

"A lot went on during the 20 years with Allen. You didn't just stay home in a depressed state."

She laughed. "I couldn't. I had two little kids, two very active little kids. Life went on despite the alcoholism. I did things despite my fatness. I went to college at night and got my bachelor's degree, and my master's degree too. It took nine years altogether, but I did it! That's what I'm really proud about. And right after I did that, I got my job."

Her voice had changed suddenly. Where it had been low, casual, and confident a moment ago, a strident, angry tone had suddenly crept in.

"Who are you mad at?"

"Me. I'm mad at me."

"Why?"

"So many years! So many years of my life unhappy because I was too scared, because I didn't have confidence in myself." Just as suddenly as it had come on, her anger evaporated. She sighed. "And Bobby, poor Bobby, never had a chance with a father like Allen and a mother like I was."

I looked at her quizzically.

"Bobby's like his father," she explained. "Treats girls like shit."

"Oh?"

"Part of that is my fault. I let his father treat me like that. I let him treat me the way his father did, yelling, swearing, putting me down all the time. I tried to discipline him when he started to treat Jane like that, but then it was too late. He told me to f . . . off."

"Pretty strong language toward a mother."

Alice looked away. "Yeah. But I probably deserved it. I wasn't much of a mother. I certainly didn't command any respect. He did as he pleased and I just cried and walked away. He started bringing his girlfriends over and loving them up in his room. Once I caught him doing it in the living room."

"What did you do?"

"Nothing. I did nothing because I was too embarrassed. Imagine! I was an embarrassed mother because he was a belligerent and spoiled child. I think he flaunted his maleness just to embarrass me. For a time he walked around naked, in front of Jane and me."

"What did you do?"

"I cried. I told Allen. He just shrugged and told me to tell him to stop. The totally uninterested look he gave me when he said that made me cry some more. Finally, Allen caught him walking around bare and he beat him up. That made Bobby stop." Alice sighed again. "Watching Allen beat up Bobby made me realize what an animal my husband had become. For some strange reason, it also made me feel very weak and very inadequate as a mother and as a person."

"Weak and inadequate?"

"Yes."

I understood. "Watching all that violence really pointed up how little control you yourself had over your child, your children, and your own life."

Alice nodded. "There is no control where there's alcohol. My mother never had control over her life. I never learned about control. Allen never had any and that's why he's alcoholic, that's why he's violent. Bobby's got no control. It's probably why he's made two kids with different girls. He bragged to me that he doesn't even like either girl. When he told me that, it opened my eyes to the fact that he had become the animal his father was." Alice looked at me with a sad, little smile. "Sad but true, I don't like my own son, but I am his mother and I'll do what I can to help him. But what I'll never do again is have him live with me." This last statement was more than a determination. It was a resolution, voiced hard and credibly.

"Do you see him?"

She shook her head. "He calls up and we talk. Never for more than a couple of minutes. I try to make small talk with him but he can't seem to do that. He's not much of a talker. Then again," she said with the same little smile, "he's not much of anything."

"What's he doing? Where's he living?"

"He works and lives with his father."

Alice's tone was telling me that she wasn't that interested in discussing Bobby anymore, that she wanted to talk about something else. I asked her.

She nodded. "It's my major concern."

"What is?"

"Men."

"There's a man in your life?"

She nodded.

"Problems with him?"

She shook her head. "With me. I'm confused."

"About what?"

"About my relationship with him. He seems so sure of himself, so sure of me. He tells me he loves me."

"And?"

"And it makes me nervous."

"Why?"

"I don't know."

"Does it give you any good feelings to know that he loves you?"

She nodded. "Of course," she said, a little impatiently. "But it makes me nervous too." Suddenly Alice stood up and started pacing. "It's my basic problem. I don't know anything about men. They're a mystery to me. Twenty-five years married to one. I even raised one. They're still a mystery." She paused. The honest, bewildered look on her face fit her words. "I'm over 40 now but sometimes when I'm with Michael I feel like I'm just going on 16."

"You feel awkward, unsure when you're with him?"

"And scared, scared that it might turn out to be serious," she cried.

"You don't want that?"

She stopped pacing, looked at me full, and yelled, "That's exactly what I want!"

"The problem is that you're not sure whether you want a serious relationship."

"I want it," she said with a kind of wail to her voice, "but I'm afraid."

"Of what?"

"I don't know."

"I suspect it might have to do with trust."

"I trust him," she said quietly.

"He makes you feel good?"

"Very good. He makes me feel like a woman. He makes me feel good about myself. He even makes me feel sexy. He makes me feel like Allen did before we were married."

"And what you can't help but think is, 'And look what happened then!'"

"Exactly!"

"He makes you feel good, very good, but not good enough to risk another disaster."

"The disaster happened because I got married."

"You don't want to marry him?"

"I'm not sure."

"What does he want?"

"He wants to marry me. He's basically a real Mr. Straight, old-fashioned, like that. He's a widower with a married daughter. He says he's uncomfortable sleeping with me and not being married. He refuses to stay at my place because Jane is there and he won't let me stay all night at his place because he thinks it sets a bad example for her."

"Sounds like he's got some pretty straightlaced ideas."

"I don't want to make him sound like a dull prude, because he's not. It's just that he's got a strong conscience." She paused, looked away. "Anyway. That's my dilemma. I don't want to lose him but right now I don't want to marry him either."

Alice didn't resolve her dilemma with me. She never returned to counseling.

Reflections

I'm very optimistic. Alice's strengths are going to pull her through. Not only does she have insight into her dynamics, but she has the determination to employ and persevere toward a fuller and more healthful life.

Her insightful way is reflected in her admission that she fed into Allen's alcoholism by her mousey submissive ways. It was reflected even more by her realization that Allen and her mother blended into the asexual demeaning and destructive person termed "alcoholic." Her insightfulness is reflected most healthfully in the fact that she was able to compartmentalize her depression. This depression was a function of her relationship with Allen and her role as a mother. She was a failure in both areas. Her fatness was a clear symptom of it.

Although she does not obsess about it, what she rues most now is that she gave Allen so many years. She has realized for a long time now that she didn't have to. She realizes now that she does have choices, that she can indeed take charge of her life if she wants to. Her metamorphasis in appearance as well as her relationship with Michael are clear indications of these newly found realizations.

Her current dilemma is also a function of her insightfulness, of her understanding that she never learned anything about men from Allen or from Bobby, a kind of Allen clone. Allen turned out to be a Mr. Hyde without the kindly Dr. Jeckyll aspect. What scares her is her inability to trust her perception of men. My best judgment is that her strengths will provide her with the courage to resolve her dilemma.

Epilogue

Almost three months passed before I received news from her. It came in the form of a terse and anxious note. "I did it. I got married. If you pray, pray it works out. If you don't pray, wish me luck."

The follow-up letter a year later was far more expansive and positively ebullient. Almost three pages long, it described her new life as full and rewarding. "Jane's life is good too. And what I'm grateful about is that she discusses her dates with me. Want to hear the best? In the past month she's started calling Michael 'Dad.' I did right to marry Michael because I feel like I've grown. What I've learned being married to Michael is that I can grow only if I'm in a loving relationship. Thought for the day, doctor: it's people who make people grow."

3

R A O U L

"She Never Loved Me."

The handwritten referral note came from the Director of Psychiatric Services. "We need a psychodiagnostic workup on Raoul Johnson. Sorry, Joe, it's not my idea. Mike Stilton has pink-slipped him." I grinned at the apology. She had known I would be irritated by the request. My views about testing are well known. While not militantly opposed to it, I am something less than a staunch advocate, especially when the testee is alcoholic. And Raoul Johnson is alcoholic. He had been admitted to our detox center a half-dozen times. Testing, I had learned, frequently engenders hostility and/or fuels the innate suspiciousness of the alcoholic client. It does little to develop rapport, and even less to enhance a relationship. Its most salient advantage is that it is efficient. One can get to know the perception, defenses, motives, and controls of a client quickly and easily. It is precisely this rationale for expediency that has irked me for years. The testing seems to be done more to meet the needs of the institution, the staff, or the tester than those of the testee.

Michael Stilton, a young and very cautious psychiatrist, had apparently just been assigned the Raoul case. If Mike had pink-slipped him, then Raoul had probably threatened suicide. By asking for testing, Mike was covering his derriere and diffusing his responsibility. Thus, if Raoul were to carry out his threat successfully, Mike could claim that he had done everything he could to fathom the motive, including having the patient tested. Testers are obligated to tell if any pre-

43

cautionary measures need to be taken, and to spell them out if they are. Mike knew that by following the tester recommendations he could effectively escape any potential finger pointing.

I crumpled up the note. The only thing positive about the request was that it came at a very propitious time. My case load had been below par for over a week. I had time to test Raoul.

Name: Raoul Johnson
Age: 36
Profession: Accountant
Tests Administered: Wechsler Adult Intelligence Test, Object Sorting Test, Thematic Apperception Test, and the Rorschach.
Observations, Physical: Raoul is a black man, about five feet, nine inches tall, and weighs approximately 160 pounds. His complexion is very light (indeed, racially white) but his hair, in both texture and color, and the shape of his nose and lips are those of a black. His face bears the scars of a severe adolescent acne with which he is still plagued. (At the time of testing, he had several large pimples on his cheeks and chin.)
Observations, Behavioral: Raoul displayed much anxiety through the testing. He swung his legs back and forth periodically and drummed his fingers on the desk incessantly. A couple of times during the administration of the intelligence test, he got up, paced around the room, and complained loudly that the test discriminated against him racially. "Everybody knows that these tests were standardized on a white honkey population," was a comment he uttered a half-dozen times.
Test Results: Raoul is currently functioning in the superior range of intelligence (I.Q. 123). What this means is that approximately 94 percent of the national population are below him in general intelligence.

Raoul's superior ability is distributed comparably in the verbal and nonverbal spheres. In the verbal sphere, his most salient strength lies in the ability to articulate, in reasoning, and in memory. In the nonverbal sphere, he displays inordinate strength in spatial relations and in the ability to manipulate others. His method of thinking can best be described as intellectualized and syntaxical. Put simply, Raoul thinks a lot. He is the idea man par excellence. The problem is that his ideas and his thinking generally are premised upon, and generated by, a perception of reality that is distorted. Raoul perceives a hostile, threatening world filled with people who, if not out to do him in, then certainly are intent on conning him for their own purposes. He is convinced that while these purposes are hidden and unclear, they have to be nefarious. Although he is a very private person, with a strong tendency toward secrecy, Raoul will freely discuss his perception of reality. He will tell you solemnly that, "It's an asphalt jungle out there, man, and everyone in it has their own little bag filled with crap to sell." He asked me what mine was. When I told him that my purpose was to help him, he assumed an ironic knowing little smile and nodded.

This suspicious perception of people is the reason that Raoul lives with the latent but constant belief that he can trust nobody. More significant still, this same perception provides him with the justification "to get them before they can get him." This "get them first" mentality does more than just keep people at a distance. It effectively isolates him from others. The isolation, in turn, prevents him from developing any meaningful relationship—something that, ironically, he wants desperately but to which he cannot admit. His self-enforced isolation, developed over many years, has resulted in the creation of very rich fantasies about women. They are so rich and rewarding that Raoul sets time aside for them.

These fantasies feed and nurture his ego, something the real world has never done, and in his view will never do. In his fantasy world, Raoul is central, the cam on which his world turns. In this world, Raoul can and does take a condescending view of people. Their function is to serve and to enhance him—whether they know it or not. This view is perfectly consistent with his inability to trust and love. As noted, he trusts nobody because nobody is worthy of his trust, of his love, and so he loves himself—to the exclusion of anyone else. In short, Raoul is a narcissist.

The fantasies have also created a series of paradoxes in his personality. Thus, while they fuel and maintain his narcissism, they also make him yearn for an intimate relationship. While he finds much reward in them, they also prevent him from developing the interpersonal skills to get close to women. The simple truth is that when Raoul relates to a woman, his only experience with which to do it comes from his fantasy life. And so in the real world he relates to women with pathetically low self-esteem and the emotional wherewithal of a child.

Raoul's constant lack of self-esteem not only with women but in most areas of his life (the exception seems to be in his work as an accountant) is attributable in no small measure to the fact that his judgment is generally poor. And it is poor because Raoul is plagued with a conscience that could best be termed "typically alcoholic."

Sometimes it governs his whole personality. At other times it is virtually nonexistent. The effect is erratic judgment. Too often Raoul makes a decision not out of choice but out of guilt. I would bet that he overtips waiters and waitresses and gives overly generous sums to neighbors who collect for the various charities and causes. But note that this same Raoul can be insensitive, cruel even, to both the waiter and the neighborhood collector. When his conscience is in remission, Raoul is capable of publicly demeaning a person without any compunction at all. Quite probably Raoul is seen by some as a socially inappropriate eccentric, and by others as a sadist. In any case, he is not held in high esteem. Raoul knows this but doesn't have any idea of why.

It is important to realize that this vacillating conscience is the result of the fact that Raoul drinks. It dominates his person when he is sober. It is virtually absent when he is drinking. A major reason he drinks himself into inebriation is precisely to inundate his conscience and to dam up the guilt that his drinking and his fantasies about women precipitate.

There is an aspect to his fantasies that I have not been able to ascertain, something about which he is so emotionally sensitive that even his percepts on the Rorschach give no clue to it. What this means is that Raoul's sense of shame about it is unconscious as well as conscious. Drink brings it out, and when drinking, he entertains and embellishes this fantasy.

The conflict and the guilt he lives with periodically make him feel as though he is being sucked into a kind of emotional quagmire. At such times, he feels very, very tired, and that he cannot cope with his alcoholism, with his ills. He sinks into an acute depression. At such times, he contemplates suicide. My best clinical judgment is that this contemplation will not be translated into reality. This judgment is based upon the fact that despite the number and severity of his problems, at heart Raoul is the consummate narcissist. Narcissists do not commit suicide.

Finally, what needs to be stressed here is that Raoul's problems, although many, are made more acute by his addiction to alcohol. Thus, his escape into fantasy is precipitated by drink. His lack of judgment, his guilt, are both compounded by it. Were he to stop drinking, he would be in a position to develop the emotional competencies to cope with himself and with others.

Diagnostic Impression: Depressive personality associated with alcoholism.

Summary: This is a 36-year-old, light-complexioned black alcoholic man who functions in the superior range of intelligence (I.Q. 123). His considerable intelligence is utilized unproductively in thought and fantasy to distort reality. Raoul's perception of a world filled with hostile, threatening people has led to a self-enforced emotional isolation. In his isolation, he fantasizes and nurtures his ego to the exclusion of everything else. Raoul has turned himself into a narcissist. Paradoxically, he yearns for intimacy. His fantasies, his narcissism, prevent him from acquiring the interpersonal skills to develop a meaningful relationship and have fostered an acutely low self-esteem. One reason that Raoul's self-esteem remains low is that his judgment is poor, and it is so because of a conscience that vacillates between scrupulousness and nonexistence. Too often Raoul makes decisions inappropriately because he makes them out of guilt and not out of choice. His alcoholism is a major reason for the vacillation of his conscience.

There is an aspect of his conscience about which he is so emotionally sensitive that his Rorschach percepts give no clue to it. Despite his conflicts and consequent depression, I see the possibility of suicide as low. My reason for thinking this is that Raoul is a narcissist.

Most people get red when they get mad. Not Michael Stilton. Even though I had worked with him for only a few months, I had learned that whenever he became upset, his physiological system worked in reverse. His face would drain of normal skin color. At this moment it looked a shade darker than gray. This abnormality might have been caused by his remarkable control over the rest of his body, in particular, his voice, which right now was coming out soft and modulated. "You don't think he's suicidal?"

I nodded. "He's not."

"How can you be so sure?"

"I'm not Stilton." I could feel my face getting red. "I wrote my reason why. He's a narcissist."

He waved his hand, palm in, back and forth in front of his face. I had always had the impression that he did that instead of bothering to say "pooh-pooh." "I just don't buy that," he said pleasantly. "How can you conclude that from what he reports he saw looking at some ink blots?"

I wanted to scream, "If you think like that then why the hell did you ask for the testing?" Instead, I kept my temper and replied coldly, "I wouldn't dignify that question with a response."

Even though his skin had now taken on the color of rich cream, he yawned. "I've put him under close observation."

Tolerance for bureaucratic hypocrisy has never been my most salient virtue. I yelled, "You did that because you knew very well he'll put in for a discharge and you'd be rid of him."

With a complacent tone he answered, "Discharge is his choice. I'm obligated to exercise my best professional judgment as to his needs."

I exploded. "Bullshit! Your order for close observation is to meet your needs, not his. Despite his problems, Raoul admitted himself because he needs and wants treatment. Your order to put him on C.O. has effectively erased any desire he had for treatment because it feeds into his belief that everybody's out to screw him. We both know, Stilton, that your need to cover your ass is a lot stronger than any need you might have to serve your patient."

Stilton slammed out. I appreciated the slam. It was honest.

Raoul asked for and was granted a discharge three days later. I thought about him periodically. Indeed, whenever I thought about the squabble, or even saw Stilton, I wondered what Raoul was doing, if his narcissism was providing him with some kind of sanity and stability, if he had his addiction under some kind of control. For some reason I wondered, too, about the striving of his personality that I had not been able to fathom and that Raoul had hidden obsessively from himself. Even though I had reexamined the test protocols, I still did not have even a glimmer as to what that striving might be. I couldn't help but wonder if he might not fall prey to it while under the influence of liquor.

All my wondering ceased several weeks later when I picked up the local newspaper and found a half-column story captioned "Child Molester Is Guilty." With positive dismay I read how Raoul had lured a ten-year-old Girl Scout who was selling cookies into his house and then proceeded to molest her sexually.

That same night I got a call from the judge who was handling the case and with whom I was fairly well acquainted. Luke O'Brien told me that he had remanded Raoul to the state hospital for 20 days' observation because he wanted more information on him before he handed down sentence. Then in a low, confidential tone, O'Brien shot me several very disparate thoughts. "I read your psychological report. I'm not one who believes in reinventing wheels. I'm for efficiency. At the same time, I don't want to intrude on professionals in other professions."

When I'm thoroughly confused by important people, I reply politely and defferentially. "Your Honor, how can I help you?"

"You know Raoul. I'd like you to see him. I have already discussed this with the Director of Psychiatric Services. She's agreed to assign him to you if you're willing to take him on."

"Your Honor, he's Dr. Stilton's patient."

"I know. She told me. She's going to make a change in the procedure this one time as a special favor to the court."

"The court." I grinned. I never cease to marvel at how smart people can effectively veneer the truth and still give you the essential meaning. Motives continue to intrigue me. I asked, "Why do you want me?"

"I liked what you wrote about Raoul and suicide. First time I ever read anything like it. Every report recommends locking up the patient. Took candor and courage to write that report. That's the kind of person I want on this case, one who will talk and recommend straight."

"I can do that. But remember, your Honor, he has to commit to sobriety before I can or will recommend anything. If you remember, I wrote that before I knew anything about any urge he had to molest kids sexually."

"I remember," O'Brien said almost cheerfully, "and I remember you alluded to that before anybody, including Raoul, knew anything about it. I was impressed, doctor. Competence, I've learned, is a very rare commodity in all professions, and that's especially true in our respective ones. Enough about all that. Will you see Raoul for the 'court'?"

I couldn't resist, and with more than a hint of facetiousness I replied. "Your Honor, I'll be pleased to see him for the court."

Luke O'Brien's response came back in kind. "I want you to know that the court is appreciative. Now doctor, with full recognition of your talents, and at the same time recognizing the utter frailty of human judgment, the question I'd like answered is, what are the chances of his molesting again?"

Charming as his sense of humor might be, the man had to know clearly what I would do and what I could do. I told him that there was no way I could answer that question definitively, and that all I could ever give him was my best clinical opinion.

His parting comment in a W. C. Fields-like tone was, "I appreciate that, doctor, as I recognize that all we can ever do in this life is give opinions about the future. We can know it absolutely only when it's become past." On that bit of sagacity, O'Brien hung up.

The next morning I reexamined Raoul's protocols, this time searching for dynamics that might give me a clue as to the severity of his need to molest. I could find nothing.

The following transcript is an edited summary of our first five meetings.

Raoul showed up early for our first appointment. He looked as I thought he would—devastated. The glazed look in his eyes blended with fear and shame. "Hi," I said cheerfully. "Remember me?"

I waited a moment, but only a moment, because my style with one who is basically suspicious is to confront. In any case, and especially in this one, I saw no point in ignoring or denying why he was in my office. "You look like hell!"

His nod told me he was indifferent to both how he looked and my chit-chat. He just stared at the landscape picture on the wall to my right. I knew he wasn't seeing it.

I had less than 20 days to get to know him, to confirm what I had found in testing. I just didn't have time to let him luxuriate in withdrawal. I plunged in. "The judge wants me to see you."

He gave me a dumb nod, and continued his unseeing stare.

"He wants me to get to know you so well that I'll be able to tell him whether or not I think you'll molest again."

His look leveled into mine and he spoke his first words. "I didn't really molest her."

I jerked back. "But you pleaded guilty."

"I didn't want a trial. Besides, I was guilty in a sense." He looked away again and became silent.

Raoul was talking in the deliberately unclear way of the untrusting, suspicious person.

"Raoul," I said evenly, "I'd really appreciate plain talk. What do you mean 'guilty in a sense'?"

His head began shaking as if he had suddenly become afflicted with Parkinson's syndrome. Moments later, with head down and in a voice that was soft and showed much bewilderment, he told me the story. Yes, he had talked the little girl into the house on the pretext that he had to get the money to pay her for three boxes of cookies. Once in the house, he told her that he wanted to give her some candy.

He stopped talking. The telling of it was just as painful for him as I had figured. I waited a few moments, and then asked gently, "Did she want the candy?"

"Yeah, she said so. She said to give her the candy." His voice had become very raspy, and was quavering.

Again he paused.

"Did you give her the candy?"

He shook his head. "I didn't have any candy to give her." He looked up at me. There were tears in Raoul's eyes. "I don't believe I did it, but I did. I did it."

"What? What did you do?"

"I dropped my pants."

"You exposed yourself?"

"I did that," he croaked, head bowed again.

"What else did you do?"

He looked up again, wiped the tears with his shirtsleeve. Because of our long chauvinistic history of cowboys, cops, and cavalry, I still have twinges of discomfort when another man cries. The empathic climate of counseling notwithstanding, I continue to experience those twinges periodically. I did so in that moment with Raoul. I looked at him and repeated my question softly, "What else did you do, Raoul."

Eyes squinched in misery, he groaned his response. "I asked her to suck it."

"Did she?"

He shook his head. "Her eyes got all big and she just ran out."

"You didn't try to stop her?"

"Christ no. I was more scared than she was."

Those words raised a very important question. If my sense was right, I'd have a lot more insight into Raoul's dynamics. "Raoul, did you have an erection?"

"When?"

"When you dropped your pants."

"No."

"Afterward?"

"After she ran out? Christ no."

"Did you at any point?"

He sighed. "Before she came to the door I was drinking."

"And daydreaming." As soon as I said it I was angry with myself. He looked at me surprised. "Yeah. How'd you know that?"

I shrugged. "Tests told me a lot. I'm sorry. I shouldn't have interrupted. Anyway, you were daydreaming."

"Yeah."

"About what?"

He shrugged. "What else?"

"Girls."

He nodded.

I leaned forward. "Now, Raoul, what kind of girls do you ordinarily dream about?" Suddenly I realized that it had been embarrassment that had kept Raoul's head down during the last several exchanges. Not atypically, my professional zeal to know and deduce the why of his behavior had gotten in the way of good professional judgment, in the way of simple human thoughtfulness. I should have realized that disclosure about his fantasies was a lot more private for him than telling about dropping his pants. Exposing himself had not been especially private because it had involved another person and it had been real. His fantasies were at the core of his private world, revealed the very essence of him.

I backed off. "My question was very private. I appreciate if you want to call it a day. We'll talk some more tomorrow."

The next day Raoul came in with more hostility than embarrassment. "Why do you have to know 'these things?' "

"About your daydreams?"

"Yeah."

"It'll tell me something about the chances of your doing it again."

"Yeah?" The tone was skepticism purified.

"Let me explain." I then summarized rapidly what I had found in his psychodiagnostic report, finishing with, "So you see, Raoul, there's a reason why I ask what I ask. Our daydreams play a big part in what we want and do."

"You know all about me." The skepticism had evaporated. He now looked at me with a wonder that embarrassed me.

I shook my head. "If I knew all about you, you wouldn't need to see me."

"Yeah," he said without conviction. "Anyway, you were asking about the kind of girls I think about."

"Yes. Can you describe them for me?"

"What do you mean?"

"Just that. Are they old, young, big, small?"

"Small," he said looking away.

"Young, old?"

"I never thought about it." Raoul had closed his eyes. That led to a question I'd thought about since we had begun the interviews. "Raoul, would you be willing to be hypnotized?"

His eyes opened wide and without the slightest pause he said, "No way!"

I grinned, had suspected he wouldn't. To be really effective, hypnosis requires a very trusting patient. Raoul was something less than that. I doubted he would ever be a hot prospect for such a process.

"O.K. Now as for the girls. Are they girls or are they women?"

Even today, a lot of people, men and women, use the terms interchangeably.

In Raoul's case I was right. "What's the difference?"

"Are these girls in their 20s, middle-aged, in their teens, or really young?"

"You asked me that already and I told you I never thought about it." Irritation had crept into his voice.

"Raoul," I said, "I know you don't like talking about this. I can never know how painful this has to be because I'm not you. Only you know that. But to be of any help to you at all I have to know who turns you on—females who are well developed or children who are not or are somewhere in between. What?"

Raoul shrugged. "I don't know what you mean."

I couldn't tell whether he was lying, emotionally resisting, or really found my question incomprehensible. "Raoul, are you attracted to tits, ass, or legs?"

Raoul's eyes widened again. He turned pink. "I'm not sure."

For some strange reason, I believed him. "You're not sure?"

He shook his head. "I like all of those. At least I look a lot when nobody's watching, but I look at, I'm attracted to, faces, I think, most of all."

"Faces?" I had trouble keeping the surprise out of my voice.

"Yeah, faces. I like kind faces."

"It's not the body that is important, it's the face?"

"Yeah. At least it is to me." Raoul said that quietly, evenly, like he meant it.

Reflections

Raoul is still suffering from the trauma of being arrested and convicted of child molestation. My sense is that he didn't actually touch the child or that the child touched him. If this is true, then what we learn is that he is so beset with guilt for luring the child into his house and exposing himself that he feels he can atone only by pleading guilty to the charge. Raoul is so ashamed of what he did that actual molestation and the act of showing his genitals to the little girl are the same for him.

Now a question, and a critical one, is, is he sexually stimulated by little girls or by women? His response of "faces" to this line of questioning intrigues me. Is it possible that Raoul is indeed attracted to faces rather than bodies? If this is true, then it means that he could conceivably molest again. A child's face could be just as, if not more, appealing to him than the face of an adult woman. Apparently Raoul emotionally (in his fantasies too?) divorces face from body. What he said, and with conviction, is that he is attracted to a kind face. My impression is that Raoul looks at and is attracted to a face that he perceives to be receptive to a relationship. The age of that face is of little consequence. His only requirement seems to be that it be the face of a woman.

I need to know more, a lot more, about how inebriated he really was while with the little girl, what experiences he's had sexually, and what sex means to him. Before these interviews, I believed his fantasies to be primarily of a sexual nature. Apparently they weren't.

"Raoul you told me that before the kid came to the door you'd been drinking."

He nodded emphatically.

"How do you feel about your drinking now?"

"It's over."

"Why should I believe that?"

"I never denied my drinking before. I don't deny now. I was a drunk. I'm not anymore."

"You're not a drunk anymore?"

"No!"

I was curious about how he was saying all this. Most alcoholics who start on the road to recovery and sobriety continue to define themselves as alcoholics, as old drunks, or in comparable terms. Raoul was not doing that. Rather, he seemed to be describing his alcoholism as a phase he had passed through, an unimportant past event, a canceled check as it were.

"Are you going to drink again?"

He shook his head. "No."

"I repeat, why should I believe that?"

"You don't have to. I know I won't."

"How do you know?"

"I know because before I never said I was going to stop drinking.

I never said that because I enjoyed drinking. I enjoyed sitting in my house drinking alone."

"Did you enjoy drinking to excess?"

"Yes," he cried.

The answer was so unusual that I believed it! "O.K.," I said quietly, "if you enjoyed it all so much, why stop?"

Raoul's eyes widened. "Why? You don't have to play any mind games with me. You know why. I really hurt that little girl. I don't know if my drinking played a part in it, it probably did. I'm just not taking any chances."

"Are you saying the booze made you do it?"

He shook his head. "No. But I am saying that if I hadn't had anything I probably wouldn't have. I'd been too scared to even try. Booze drowns my fears. It has for a lot of years. In fact, if I hadn't had anything to drink, I probably wouldn't have even thought of it."

I tended to agree with that assessment. It fit the test findings. Drink precipitated a lot of his fantasies. In any case, there's little doubt that the booze had lowered his control. His next words confirmed my thoughts.

"I'd been drinking for about two hours. I wasn't blotto, but I wasn't feeling too much pain. I was feeling mellow, which was the feeling I really liked, the one I aimed for every time I drank, which was every day. Like I said, I enjoyed drinking."

"You enjoyed drinking." I repeated his remark because I was try-ing to sort out what he was saying to me. For some reason, I believed him when he said he would drink no more. At the same time, his comments about enjoying drink confounded that belief.

"Yeah, I did. I come from a long, long line of drinkers. My pa used to say that Johnsons were hard drinkers."

"Your father was a hard drinker?"

"Yeah."

"And your mother?"

"She didn't drink at all."

"I see. How did they get along?"

"All right, I guess. At least they never got divorced."

I asked about his childhood.

He told me he was an only child and had grown up in a small town in northern Virginia. His father worked for the railroad. He described his mother as very strict. She was an elementary school teacher. "Pa's work kept him away for two, three days in a row. Then he'd be home for almost a week. I used to hate to see him go to work."

He had told me enough to give me an idea of the possible why of his problems.

"Why? Why did you hate to see him go to work?"

"Because I liked him."

"What about your mother? Did you like her?"

"Yeah, I liked her." He said that testily.

I pressed. "But you liked your father more?"

"What if I did?"

"Why did you like him more?"

"I don't know why, maybe because he was more relaxed."

"Your mother wasn't?"

"She was a teacher."

I chuckled. "Teachers are not relaxed."

Raoul shot me an angry look. "You're putting words in my mouth."

"Tell me about your mother."

"What's this got to do with anything?"

"Maybe a lot. I want to know what it was like for you at home."

"I told you."

"So far, all you have told me is that your father was away a lot and that your mother was a school teacher who wasn't as relaxed as your father."

"She was lonely. Her family came from Alabama. Pa's family lived near us. I didn't see them much because ma didn't get along with them."

"Why not?"

"I think she thought she was better than them. Pa's folks were poor. They were farmers who lived a couple of miles outside of town. I didn't really know what dirt poor meant until I visited them after my father died. Both my grandparents are still alive and they're living in the same place they've always lived in. It's a shack, a real shack, not even painted. My father used to take me there sometimes on weekends. I liked going there because there was a lot of laughter, a lot of noise. Aunts and uncles used to come. I had kids to play with. It was fun."

"You said your mother thought she was better than them."

"Yeah." Raoul paused. "That's ma's problem. She still thinks like that. She lives all alone in an apartment now. Never sees anybody. She has no friends. She has no friends because she thinks she's better than everybody. When I was a kid, I had nobody to play with because ma thought nobody was good enough to play with me."

Raoul smiled ironically.

"Like I told you, ma was a teacher, the only black teacher in town. She felt like she had to set an example."

"Set an example? For whom?"

"For everybody. For blacks, and whites too."

"Growing up, I was the best kid there ever was because I was her little example."

"Were you teased a lot because of it?"

"Christ no. There never was anybody around to tease me."

"What about in school?"

"I was the only black kid in the elementary school. We lived in the white section of town."

"Didn't you play with kids before or after school?"

He shook his head. "I used to go to school with my mother and I came home with her."

"Every day?"

He nodded. "Just about."

"How did you feel about that?"

"I didn't. I didn't feel anything about it. I just accepted it. Like I told you, I was her little example."

"And by the time you became her big example you had become a confirmed loner."

"You got it. And by that time I got to feeling so different from both blacks and whites that I swear to God I felt like I had come from another planet."

"So you grew up feeling very different?"

"Yeah. Ma never saw anything wrong with how she brought me up. Still doesn't. The sad part of it all was that nobody cared about who we were or what we were anyway. The black people on the other side of town were too poor, too ignorant, to care if we were important, and the white people, rich or poor, educated or ignorant, looked down on us because we were black. Meanwhile, I was brought up like I had a contagious disease, or I'd get one if I went near anybody."

Raoul stopped talking, looked away, then looked back at me and sighed. "But there's another reason I grew up feeling different. Didn't have to do with how my mother brought me up."

"What reason?"

"How I look."

The puzzlement I showed was genuine. "How you look?"

"Not black, and not white either."

"People tease you about that?"

He shook his head. "No, but I could see I didn't look either white or black."

"When did you start to notice that?"

"I'm not sure. I think somewhere around the fifth grade. I noticed that my lips were thicker than those of any kid in my class but my skin was just as white. Then one time, one time only, a kid made a comment in the school yard. I was watching two kids scaling baseball cards against the wall and this new kid came up to me and asked, and not in a mean way either, 'You white or colored?' I never forgot that."

"It was the question you'd been asking yourself."

He nodded. "That question haunted me."

"Does it today?"

He shook his head. "No. I've learned to be black, but like everything all my life, it came slowly because I've never been with black people that much—I guess any people. But as a kid it was awful for me. I wanted to be white but I didn't admit that to myself. I just figured that out lately, when I think about it. You know how I figured it out?"

"How?"

"I got so I was ashamed of my parents, both of them. I didn't want to be seen with them because they were ten shades darker than me. You know that line about being from another planet? I realize now I said that before because when I was a kid, I got so I sometimes thought that or wished it. I used to daydream about being from Krypton. Weird huh?"

I shook my head. "Not weird at all. Kids fantasize a lot."

"I wasn't that much of a kid anymore when I was doing that. I was in junior high and high school. Christ, I was doing it even when I was in college."

"You've led a very lonely life."

"For sure."

"And since you didn't have anybody to turn to, you turned in on yourself. Your fantasy about being from some mythical planet was the way to get some esteem. People from other planets may be weird, but they are special too. Krypton gave us Superman. Anyway, you were saying you got to the point that you started to become ashamed of your parents. You didn't want to be seen with them."

"Especially as a teenager. I always found an excuse not to go with my father on Sundays to see my grandparents and relatives."

"Because being with them confirmed the fact that you were black."

"Yeah, and I never admitted that to myself. I didn't have to. I had my mother's support not to go. If my father nagged me about going, she'd say 'Leave the boy alone. He's got to do his work for school.' Or 'He's reading. It's much more important that he read than it is for him to visit those people outside of town.' She always referred to pa's folks as 'those people,' like they were trash. Once he said it, and just like that too, 'Emma, when you say those people, you make it sound like you're saying the word trash.'"

"What did she say?"

"She denied it or she ignored it. One of the two, because that's how she treated him. In thinking about it now, I guess she also treated him a little like he was trash."

Refections

I'm inclined to do so but still am not sure I can believe that Raoul will adhere to his resolution to stop drinking. There is no doubt at all that he is horrified about what he did and desperately wants to atone for it. But whether he will be able to live with his guilt rather than periodically anesthesizing it with alcohol remains to be seen. In any case, his resolution is not only an encouragement, but, as already noted, it is an indispensable prerequisite to his rehabilitation.

What these last sessions have also told us is that Raoul's upbringing was an unmitigated disaster. Raoul has lived most of his life in a state of crisis identity. A father who was absent too much and who was ignored and belittled when present was hardly an ideal role model. Even so, Raoul identified more with him than with his mother because she was totally depriving. Classically overprotective, she took over his ego and made him her "little example," a real mama's boy. With little or no sense of self, he felt so ashamed, so different, that he sought desperately for some kind of identity. The search became all consuming. It became the springboard that launched his fantasy life. It took him to mythical planets. It spanned his childhood, teen, and adult years. Ironically, this same search for identity was what deprived him of contact with people, role models from whom he could have learned and acquired a better sense of his own self.

There is still much denial operating in this personality, which still functions in an alcoholic-like fashion. My sense is that he continues to deny much about the parental relationship. And this man/woman relationship is the only one to which he was ever close enough to observe, the only one apparently from which he learned and mislearned. I need to explore this relationship further.

"What I've been wondering about since our last session is how your parents got along."

"Yeah?"

"You said that your mother treated him a little like trash."

"Yeah."

"Did she do that a little bit or a lot?"

Raoul sighed. "A lot. She did it a lot."

"She looked down on him?"

He nodded. "My father wasn't a high school graduate. She used to say that."

"I presume she said it to put him down?"

"What else? Ma nagged a lot."

"Him? You? Who?"

"Both of us. Him more."

"Did they fight a lot?"

He nodded. "A lot when I was small. Not much when I was older, when I was in high school. I guess pa got tired as he got older. I'm not sure, but I think he drank a lot more then."

"Raoul, was he alcoholic?"

Raoul shrugged. "He's dead now."

"Not what I asked," I said, the impatience in my voice apparent, on purpose. I paused, decided to confront. "You say you're not going to drink anymore but you talk like an alcoholic."

His confused look was honest. "What do you mean by that?"

"You deny that you're alcoholic and that your father was."

"I'm not denying anything" he protested. "I admit that I drank too much. And I told you that my father drank too much. I even told you that Johnsons have always been hard drinkers."

Raoul's denial was summed up in his aversion to the word "alcoholic." Sometimes therapy can become painful. I was feeling the pain because I knew he was. I continued with my confrontation. "Can you say the word, Raoul?"

"What word?"

The awful tragedy had suddenly taken on a crazy, comic flavor. Raoul was not playing any games. His confused, bewildered expression told me that this person who functioned in the superior range of intelligence honestly could not figure out what word I meant. Such is the power of denial. My sense also was that he was operating under some kind of misguided notion that he would be disloyal to his father and to the tradition of hard-drinking Johnsons if he used the word to describe his and their condition.

What I had known for a whle but completely realized only then was that, at some level, Raoul was very aware of the fact that the only paternal aspect with which he had been able to identify had been the "hard drinking." Were he now to label that hard drinking as alcoholism, he would be saying that the only thing he got from his father was a disease. Still worse, he would have to strip himself of the only visible "masculine" aspect of his father. All this had to be very frightening for Raoul because, consciously or unconsciously, he knew that his health lay in adding to his sense of identity and not in stripping any more away from it.

I wouldn't utter the word for him. It had to come from him. Insight is not a lesson. It cannot be imparted. I waited. It was worth it.

Raoul yelled, "Why is it so important to say that I'm alcoholic and I come from a long line of alcoholics? Tell me why that's so important?"

The tears in Raoul's eyes were very real. And, even though I knew I had been quite correct to press him so hard, at that moment I felt more like an unsuccessful sadist than an effective psychotherapist. Even so, I couldn't, wouldn't, let him manipulate me into telling him what we both knew he knew. "Raoul, you've been in enough group sessions here at detox to know the answer to those questions."

Raoul closed his eyes, and in a voice that reminded me of a grade-schooler reciting his lesson, said, "We admitted we were powerless over alcohol—that our lives had become unmanageable. Admission of powerlessness is the first step in liberation. Is that it, doc? Is that what you want me to say?"

I shook my head. "Unimportant what I want you to say. But what I noticed is that you said all that like it was in your head, not in your heart."

He gave me a little ironic grin. "Probably is. I have never been able to get into the AA philosophy."

"Some people can't. What you have to get into is a clear sense of your own purpose."

"I'm into myself. Probably too much," he said in a very quiet voice.

"I don't mean being preoccupied with yourself. What I'm talking about is seeing yourself for what you are, for who you really are."

"I'm not sure I know what that means."

I nodded. "O.K. It's what I was trying to get at before. What and who you are has to do with what and who you came from."

He grimaced. "Back to my ma and pa."

I nodded. "Right."

He sighed. "O.K."

"What I'm especially interested in is what you barely got started on before, namely, on how your parents got along."

"They didn't. When I was little, they had some real loud and nasty fights, and always at night. They'd wake me up fighting. Later on, they didn't fight, hardly at all." Raoul gave a funny, tight-lipped chuckle. "Probably because they barely talked to each other. By the time I was in high school ma and pa didn't talk."

"What did you all do in the house?"

"Not much. Ma read a lot. Pa drank a lot. He watched TV in the living room."

"What about you, Raoul? What did you do?"

"I sat in my room."

"You sat in your room?"

"Yeah."

Raoul bent his head and was silent for a few minutes. Suddenly he looked up brightly. "Yeah. I sat in my room."

His sudden new resistance was not a function of hostility but of acute pain—the most common denominator among alcoholics. Pressing via confrontation only increases that pain. I stayed silent, waited. Several more minutes passed.

"You know what I did?"

"Tell me."

"I listened to the radio."

There was another protracted pause.

"You know why I did that?"

I shook my head.

"I did that because I couldn't stand being in the living room watching TV with my father, watching him get himself polluted every night."

Raoul's voice had suddenly taken on a detached, hollow tone. There was no emotion there. He was finally broaching the reality of his father's alcoholism, was even admitting to it but was doing it through intellectualization, in a purely objective mental way. Even though his words held more than a little resentment and bitterness, the emotion on which those words rode was flat. Even though the words were those of a hurt son, the tone could have been that used by a social worker describing a client.

I addressed the tone. "How did it make you feel watching your father getting polluted?"

He shrugged. "It was his life."

I repeated my question. "How did it make you feel?"

His shoulders slumped suddenly. "Scared. It made me feel scared." Raoul paused. "I don't think I saw a TV show after I entered high school because he'd just plunk down in front of it after supper and drink till he passed out. I tried watching TV with him because I wanted to. And I did in grade school and in junior high, but I stopped. You know why I stopped?" Raoul's voice had lost all its detachment. It became filled with sorrow.

"Why did you stop?"

"One night he was drinking much faster than usual. He'd gone through his first six-pack before my eight o'clock program had even begun. I tried to wake him and help him to bed like I'd seen a kid do in an old movie. The movie scene was funny. The scene I lived through was tragic. I called him softly, then louder and louder. Then I started slapping him on the face, little soft slaps like I'd seen the kid do in the movie. Suddenly he opened his eyes and slammed me hard on the side of the head. He hit me so hard that I ended up on the other side of the room. Then he started kicking and screaming at me. 'Don't you never hit your daddy again. Never, never, never.'

With every 'never,' he gave me a kick. My mother came running in shrieking, 'stew bum, no-account stew bum.' He stopped kicking but I swear ma never stopped shrieking. She went on for hours."

Raoul paused for a few moments. Then in a voice edged in tears he rasped, "I never forgot that scene, and I guess I never will. You know why?"

"Why?"

"Because what I realized even when it was all happening was that ma didn't care all that much that he beat me up. What she didn't like was that it happened in her house because it's not proper to beat your kid up."

"Why do you say that?"

"Because she never held me or comforted me afterward. She just sent me to bed with words to the effect that we both had to make the best of it because he was a no-account stew bum." Raoul shook his head. "Never a hug or a kiss or anything, just a pat on the head— and an apology."

"Apology?"

"Yeah. She apologized for screaming. It wasn't proper to scream. After that night she used that phrase 'stew bum' a lot."

"Because he beat you up so much?"

Raoul shook his head vehemently. "Christ no! That's probably why I remember it all so much. He never hit me, not before that night, or after either.

"You know, I think that, crazy as it sounds, she was kind of glad that he beat me up like I was an animal because it gave her an excuse to call him a stew bum. It gave her the excuse she was looking for to treat him like trash."

I nodded. "Proper people don't beat up their kids. He beat you up. He wasn't proper. He was trash."

"Exactly what she thought. That's how she still thinks, I'm sure. You know, doc, more than 20 years have gone by since that night and I'm still hurt that she didn't comfort me. I've asked myself a thousand times why I'm hurt about that time because she never hugged or kissed me anyway. Why should I be hurt?"

Although his question was framed in honest puzzlement, I knew he knew the answer. It just hurt too much to admit to it.

"Tell me," I said gently, "was your father a hugger and a kisser?"

"Naw! He was a man, and besides he was drunk all the time, if that's an excuse."

"He had an excuse."

"Yeah."

"And she didn't. Is that what you're thinking, feeling maybe?"

Raoul looked up, eyes brimming. In that split second all the deprivation and hurt of his childhood were mirrored on his face. The look was so utterly real in its pathos, communicated so eloquently, that I suddenly wanted to hold him myself. Apparently my own feelings were showing too, because Raoul's tears spilled over and literally flowed. I went over and put my arm around his shoulder.

Head down, he sobbed. "She never loved me. She never loved me. My own mother never loved me!" I kept my arm around his shoulder for a long while. It was at this same session, while he was leaving, that Raoul made another most telling observation, another acutely painful admission. This time, however, it was without tears. "Before you said that who I am has to do with what and who I come from. I guess what I've always felt about myself is that I'm not much because I don't come from much."

Then, surprisingly and unaccountably he put on a little smile and gave me a wink. "I'm going to have to work on that, eh?"

I nodded. "For sure."

Reflections

Raoul's parents taught him much, albeit nothing positive. From his mother he learned that women are cold, condescending, and indifferent.

What he learned from his father is that a real man drinks to excess and is not supposed to communicate affection. From their relationship he learned that women are infinitely more competent than men, that they are powerful and are in charge of the male/female relationship. He learned too, through his mother's condescension and indifference, that women can be devastatingly cruel.

In sum, not only did he not learn anything from either parent about the giving and taking of affection, but just as bad, he learned that the male/female relationship is not enhancing for a man, and can be demeaning. Relationships, he learned, are a source of pain, certainly not something to seek out. These lessons had two very unfortunate effects: They militated against the acquisition of any interpersonal skills, and they became the reason for his unconscious understanding that fantasy was preferable to reality.

At this point, I felt I had enough information and knew Raoul well enough to give Judge O'Brien my best clinical opinion. I wrote my report and had it delivered to his chambers, a half-mile from my hospital office.

The call came within an hour. "This is Luke O'Brien. How are you?"

"Just fine. Yourself?"

"Just fine. Just fine. Doctor, I was calling not only to inquire after your health, but also to discuss your report, and even as I talk I realize that the phone is not the most suitable medium for doing so. Could you possibly fit me into your luncheon schedule?"

I grinned. O'Brien had to be the only man I knew who could be deferential and aggressive at the same time. I answered him in the way I knew he wanted. "Oh I think I might manage to squeeze you in."

"When?"

"Today, if you like."

"I'm grateful. Noon O.K.?"

"O.K."

"I'll have you picked up then."

Promptly at 12 a young deputy sheriff was at my office door to drive me to the judge's chambers in the courthouse.

The judge greeted me at the door. O'Brien fits the stereotype I have of what a judge is supposed to look like. He dresses in expensive, dark, pin striped suits. Over six feet tall and heavy, he wears his thick mane of startlingly white hair a little longer than is fashionable. He led me to a side table on which lay a variety of sandwiches, salads, and dessert goodies.

I had eaten less than a quarter of my sandwich before he turned his blue-eyed gaze on me. "I liked your report, doctor. It was what I expected. Straightforward. But I want to talk about it." He looked at me and, with no facetiousness whatsoever, said in a soft voice, "I need counsel on this."

I chewed the excellent roast beef slowly. "What did I not say that you'd like to know?"

"You said," he noted, looking at a pad, "that the potentiality for future molestation is minimal."

I nodded.

O'Brien leaned forward, eyes disturbingly direct. He said crisply, "If you were booking, what odds would you give against the fact that he would molest another kid."

I leaned back and grinned. "No offense, your Honor, but that's something less than a scientific method of assessment."

O'Brien didn't grin back. "Maybe. But it's one I use in comparable cases. Helps me understand better. Helps me make decisions with less conflict. Your best clinical judgment, doctor. What are your 'bookmaker's odds.' "

Only O'Brien could make terms like 'clinical judgment' and 'bookmaker's odds' sound perfectly compatible. I swallowed. "Alright, if he gives up drinking, as I think he will, I'd give 20 to one that he won't molest again. If he drinks, all bets are off."

"You think he'll stop drinking?"

"Yes, because he's aware that it might have contributed to the whole sordid incident, and he's more horrified than anyone else about what he did. And the truth is, he didn't actually molest that little girl." I recounted the story and finished with, "I believe it all."

O'Brien nodded, "O.K."

"Your Honor, whatever you decide to do, I recommend that you not mandate him into counseling. To mandate him into counseling is like mandating the proverbial horse to drink."

O'Brien's look was an attentive one. Little doubt that he was listening. I left hopeful.

Two days later I received word from a probation officer that Raoul had been sentenced to three years in jail, sentence suspended. The suspension was contingent on his accepting placement in a halfway house for the rehabilitation of alcoholics. Before noon that same day, I received another call from Luke O'Brien. His voice was cheerful. "You heard?"

"I heard."

"What do you think?"

I replied honestly. "Sounds good."

"You're not peeved with me?"

"Peeved? Why should I be peeved?"

"One of my conditions of the suspension was that he go into treatment with one of our more celebrated therapists."

"I told you that mandated therapy is just not . . ." I stopped, realizing that my thoughts and opinions were now irrelevant.

His voice still cheerful, but now with just a hint of analgesia in it, he said, "I heard everything you told me but you have to realize that I just can't release a man to society without a gilt-edged assurance to my conscience that I've structured for the best probability of success. And doctor, lest you think I don't, I know full well about horses and drinking water. I decided to leave his motivation to get well in part to you."

I felt my irritation moving rapidly toward fury. "Suppose I don't agree to this grand scheme?"

The reply was instant "He goes to jail."

I wanted to yell, "You lousy blackmailing, dictatorial son of a bitch!" Instead I said nothing, sputtered something about how I had to think about it. I spent more than a few moments trying to regain my calm. Then the line I bank on to untangle my thinking when I become enmeshed in petty squabbling about clients came to me, "Whose needs am I trying to meet?" As usual, the question put me back on track. I called O'Brien back, and was even able to inject humor in my tone. "O.K., you talked me into it, your Honor."

To Raoul, who had always lived life in aloneness, the halfway house was initially very threatening. It abounded with people. For weeks Raoul, shy and with few interpersonal skills, moved in a state of bewilderment.

Our therapy sessions during those first weeks focused on that bewilderment. His major complaint was that he had no privacy, that he was scheduled into too many activities, and that people talked too much.

"You want to be alone more."

"Yeah. That's what I want."

Again and again over those first sessions I pointed out, and in a variety of ways, that it was precisely his desire to be alone that had fueled his fantasies, shaped his view that people couldn't be trusted, kept him in a state of interpersonal immaturity.

It took a long time, six months of living with others, and almost six months of sessions with me and in group, before Raoul was able to make the admission for which I had been waiting.

It was his opening remark of the session, and he said it even before he sat down. "You know what made me sick all these years?"

I pointed to his chair and asked, "What?"

"Being by myself. Being by myself. That's what did it."

What I never cease to marvel at is that clients invariably make these critically important observations as if they had never been discussed and had just been discovered by them. We call this insight.

"When did you arrive at the bit of wisdom?"

"Last night. Last night."

"Anything happen to . . . ?"

"Went to the dinner-dance. And you know what? You know what?"

"What?"

"I danced!" The wonder in his voice was real. So was the happy little glow in his eyes. The message was clear, and his next words confirmed it. "I met this great woman."

Then, because he so wanted me to, I said, "Tell me about her."

Raoul rattled on happily for many minutes describing and exclaiming the virtues of Claudia. I felt a little as though I were listening to a naive adolescent who had just discovered the opposite sex, or who *knew* he had found the person with whom he was going to have an eternally meaningful relationship.

Within a few weeks, Raoul was depressed. Claudia had broken up with him. His depression, however, was shortlived. That told me that his self-esteem was rising. Apparently Raoul felt confident that he could find another woman, that he could develop another relationship. Subsequent events were to prove him correct; in the next year, Raoul met and romanced a half-dozen women. The focus of these sessions was a function of the current state of his relationships. And his relationships vacillated between blissful and nonexistent. I couldn't determine if the constant vacillations were going to be long term or if he was just passing through some kind of adolescent phase.

During this same phase, Raoul was discharged from the halfway house, and found an apartment and a new job as an accountant.

He asked to see me at the hospital on an outpatient basis. Our sessions continued to focus on his relationships with women, his abiding concern. Interestingly, he seemed to find little trouble in developing solid relationships at work as he was promoted twice in his first year on the job.

His success with people at work was a hopeful sign. However, I learned long ago that success with people on the job does not necessarily reflect or make for success in intimate relationships.

After each breakup, Raoul would come out with the same plaintive whine, "Why can't I make it with a girl long term?"

I never answered that question because I didn't know why. I was as puzzled as he was, and thought about it a lot. Raoul was not unattractive physically. Indeed, he was probably more attractive to women now than when we had started our sessions as he had been treated successfully for the acne condition he had endured during most of his life. And even though he lacked heterosexual experience, Raoul was not boring. Why then the periodic breakups?

Once in response to the inevitable plaintive whine, I asked, "Are you being yourself with them?"

"What does that mean?"

"Do you confide?"

"Confide what?" he asked in a transparently defensive tone.

"About yourself, your drinking, your experience in the halfway house and why it happened."

"Talking about those things is being myself?"

"Yes. Sharing yourself gets people closer. Do you do that?"

He shook his head. "No. But I listen good. They've all told me that."

"You don't have to trust to listen. You have to trust to share yourself. What I'm beginning to realize is that you haven't found a woman yet in whom you can trust and confide."

Raoul didn't respond. However, I had the impression that he had listened. My impression proved right because not six months later Raoul was married.

Epilogue

He's kept in touch, by telephone mostly. Last month, on the occasion of his third wedding anniversary, he sent me a card. "Wanted to let you know we had a baby ten days ago. I had a thought I wanted to share. I had it the first time I held my son. *Takes an awful lot of trust to have a baby.* Thanks, doc."

4

B E T T Y

"Whores Don't Have Relationships!"

Auburn-haired, green-eyed, and full-bodied, Betty stands about five feet five. She's the kind of woman men always notice, and after noticing, want to stare at. I didn't stare, but I had to expend a lot of energy to look elsewhere. We were in the cafeteria line at a local manufacturing company where I consult. She was two people behind me. I felt her direct glances as I chose my food. Betty was at my table before I sat down.

"May I join you, doctor?"

I nodded to the opposite chair. "Please. I hate to eat alone." That's true, and truer still that my lunch is always interesting. In this plant setting, once people know who you are and what you do, there is no scarcity of dining companions. At the same time, most people who ask to eat lunch display a little nervousness, embarrassment about doing so. Betty, a middle manager in finance, did not. She chatted in a relaxed way about people she knew I had to know in Personnel and Health Services. Halfway through her tuna salad, she said, "I'd like to make an appointment with you."

I told her I was booked solid, that my commitment to the plant was five hours per week, and all five hours were full.

"I know," she said, "Hilda told me." Hilda is my appointment secretary in the plant. "Could you see me privately?"

That I could do.

"Can you tell me a little about the problem now?"

She looked at me and sighed. "I think I need to get a divorce but I don't want to. I just don't want to." She said all that in a muted tone, and with just a hint of eyebrow flutter.

"I'm confused. Why do you need to, if you don't want to?"

"I don't want to because I've already had two divorces. I'm 25 years old and I'm on my third marriage. Sick, eh?"

"I don't know if it's sick, but it sounds like there are problems."

"What you're saying is I could use some counseling," she said with a laugh.

I nodded. "Have you ever had any?"

She shook her head. Three divorces and never any counseling. It was unusual. I didn't comment.

A week later I saw her. She showed up promptly, was in the waiting room when I opened the connecting office door. She wore a pale-green suit, tightly skirted. I smelled the perfume as she brushed by, subtle, expensive. Dress and grooming fit with the sense I already had of her—classy, sophisticated, but with a penchant for seductiveness. I waved her to the big recliner and sat down in my own.

"You're having marital problems?"

"You name them, we've got them."

"So name them for me."

She shrugged. "Money, sex, caring. Those enough?"

I nodded. They were indeed enough. What I found especially curious was how she had summarized the problems, with caring coming last. I addressed that. "No love in your marriage?"

"No!"

"You don't feel he loves you?"

"I don't know if he loves me. I don't think I love him."

"You think you don't love him?"

She nodded.

"How long have you been married?"

"This time about a year. The first one lasted about three years, the second one a little under two years. They're getting shorter and shorter. Sick, eh?"

It was the second time she had posed that question, and just like that. I ignored it. "Did you love him when you married him?"

"I thought I did."

"Why don't you tell me about your first two husbands." I was getting a funny, queasy feeling about this woman and I already had a thought about her that I did not like.

"What's to tell?"

"Who they were. What they did. Why you broke up, the whole ball of wax."

Betty proceeded to tell me that she'd been married the first time at the age of 19 to a man eight years her senior. "I've always enjoyed older men. They make me feel important. They know how to act. Men my age have always seemed childish to me."

"But you fell out of love with this man. Is that right?"

She nodded. "When I married him he was exciting. He got to be the original Mr. Boring real fast."

"How fast?"

She shrugged. "I don't know—a month, a couple of months, a year. Who remembers?"

"And your second husband?"

"I wished I hadn't married him the day after we got married."

"Why?"

"He was a womanizer. He was unfaithful from the start. I should have known. He was married when I met him."

"You mean you were in an affair with him before you married him? Were you married?"

Her answer came back like a shot. "No. Of course not."

"Did you know he was married?"

"Of course I didn't know he was married." The reply, again shot back, seemed sanctimonious. For some reason, I didn't believe it. Then she added a question that set me to thinking for the rest of the next several sessions. "What do you think I am?"

Unusual for me, but I did it. I replied without thinking, and I was glad of it. "I don't know. What are you?"

Her head jerked back. "Well, I'm not a tramp. I don't enjoy being the other woman. I don't get my kicks out of breaking up marriages. I'm perfectly capable of getting my own man."

The last line had been framed in arrogance but I believed it, and I told her, "I'm sure that's true." Her reply to that was a smile. Probably because throughout the session I had sensed that she had an acute need for me to like and believe her. I filed that thought away. "Now," I said crisply, "tell me some more about these two first husbands."

She told me that the second, like the first, was older, by nine, maybe ten years. The first was a school teacher, the second a pharmacist. She had children with neither. "Did you want kids?"

"God no!"

"And you don't want any now?"

"No way."

I grinned. "You sound a little like they're a curse, or at least something to avoid."

Betty replied quickly. "Well, doctor, obviously I haven't met a man yet who satisfies me as a father." She seemed totally oblivious to what she had said as she continued to talk. "I mean a man who is a father, who wants to be a father, who finds satisfaction in the role of father, that man is a rare commodity." I started to get the same queasy feeling I'd had before because, as she talked, I had the distinct impression that she wasn't addressing me as a psychotherapist but rather the me whom she knew enjoyed being a father. My impression, too, was that she was aware of what she was saying, but only in the dimmest way. Despite my queasy feeling, or perhaps because of it, dynamics like these fascinate me. I leaned back, put a nice little grin on my face, and fed into them, obliquely. Rather than asking about her father, I asked about her parents. Her response was much what I was expecting.

She smiled, nodded. "I'm an only child and the product of a broken home. My parents were divorced when I was five."

"So you don't remember much about . . . ?"

She waved her hand as if to shush my interruption. "I can remember only four experiences while my parents were together. I remember spending Sundays at my grandparents, my father's parents. I remember being stung by a bee on my thumb before I could even walk and my father kissing it and sucking on it. I remember the giant Sugar Daddy candy stick my father kept on top of one of the kitchen cabinets. He would reward me on my good days by chiseling off a piece for me after supper. I also remember the last night we three spent together in that house. I was huddled in a bed in a corner while my parents fought until my mother pushed my father down the stairs. My father was drunk."

"Was he an alcoholic?"

She nodded. "Yes he was, and he was also kind and loving and gentle and giving and he loved me very much, the only person who ever did."

My first thought on hearing those words was the Shakespearean line, "Methinks thou doth protest too much." Why? Because alcoholic parents who are kind, loving, gentle, and giving are rare birds, or at least a curiosity. She was denying. Had to be. Now that would *not* be a curiosity but perfectly consistent with the dynamics of a child of an alcoholic. What little I had heard so far told me that Betty's dynamics were not only common, but positively textbook like. Betty's next words told me that she was aware of that.

"And I know what you're thinking."

"What?"

"That I have a father complex."

I nodded. "Something like that."

She shrugged. "People have told me that. I don't care. I like it if that's what I have. But that's not my problem."

It's always important to know how your clients see their problem. "Tell me, Betty, what's the problem?"

"I can't seem to love anybody, young or old, for any length of time. I lose interest. After a while, they're all boring to me."

"You've never had a relationship that lasted?"

"Never."

Betty sat up suddenly, crossed one long, slim leg over the other, and began to swing it slowly and rhythmically. "I've never found a man whom I could respect for any length of time. All the men I ever married married me for my looks—to be blunt about it, for sex."

"No one married you for you?"

"Exactly!" She gave me a little smile, maintained the slow rhythmic leg swinging.

I asked the question slowly. "And you, Betty, what did you marry them for?"

The surprise on her face was genuine but her reply was quick. "I married them for love that I never got."

I remembered what she had just recounted, and while painfully candid and confrontative, I felt I had to ask. "And you, Betty, have you given them love?"

Staring hard at me, she replied. "I gave them what they were looking for and expected."

She wasn't answering my question and she knew it. I asked softly, "But was it love, Betty?"

She uncrossed her legs and replied stubbornly. "They call it that. We all call it that. If you don't know, doctor, the term is 'making love'."

"Are sex and love the same thing?"

"To most people, yes."

I leaned back in my chair wondering why the sudden evasiveness, why she couldn't admit to the same values that all her husbands had. I pressed her. "And to you, are sex and love the same?"

"I never thought about it."

I believed her.

"A little while ago, you told me that your problem was the fact that you can't seem to love anybody for any length of time."

"That's right. And damn it," she cried, "I want to. I do."

Her plaintive cry seemed genuine. "Tell me, would you say you were a one-man woman?"

Betty chuckled. "Doctor, my track record seems to show I'm not."

"The question is, Betty, do you want to be?"

"I told you that I want a relationship, and I do."

I had a sudden inkling as to an important part of the why of Betty's problem. "Betty, you say you want a long-term meaningful relationship but you can't seem to answer the question I just asked."

She smiled sweetly. "Which is?"

I didn't smile back. "Do you want to be a one-man woman?"

She nodded. "If I find the right man, yes."

At that moment I would have said she fully expected not to. I debated a moment, then asked slowly. "Do you expect you will find that man?"

"He's out there somewhere I'm sure."

She said that in a tone that was something less than convincing.

Reflections

Betty is a strikingly beautiful woman who is very aware of herself and the effect she has on men. My impression, though tentative, is that she herself is alternately attracted to and repelled by them. Another impression, tentative also, is that she is quite unable to make a true commitment to any man, at least at this time. She just doesn't know what she wants from a man. Despite her sophistication and her apparent poise, Betty is a very confused person. Her query "sick, eh?" if nothing else, tells us that she is aware that she has problems. Her spontaneous cry "well, I'm not a tramp" would seem to support the notion that these problems are rooted in self-perception.

Another impression, and a strong one (indeed, it was the source of my queasy feelings), is that Betty's prime mode, maybe the only mode for relating to a man, is sexual. It is to seduce him, if not literally, then figuratively; that is, to get him to do what she wants. And she had been successful. Without a doubt, Betty is the recipient of an infinite number of favors from admiring male supervisors, tradesmen, mechanics, professionals of all kinds, and so forth. Such a mode of relating tells us that she views men as being there to be manipulated and to serve her. A very strong impression, too, is that after seducing a man, she loses all interest and whatever respect she might have had for him. The problem here is that her high rate of success in seductive/interaction reinforces her basic notion that men are only good for one thing—sex.

These thoughts lead me to think that while she complains about the infidelity of her former spouses, she has probably engaged in extramarital affairs of her own.

Among the prime topics to be discussed yet are her father and her current husband.

"We really haven't talked about your present marriage. You told me the problems had to do with money, sex, and caring."

She nodded. "The problem is that we don't have any of the three."

"Does your husband work?"

"He hasn't been working for over two months now." She went on to tell me that he was a mechanical engineer with a master's degree.

"Why doesn't he work?"

"He was fired from his last two jobs."

"Why?"

"He's alcoholic. Nobody around here will hire him now. They all know about him."

I was curious so I began slowly. "Betty, he must have been alcoholic for a . . ."

She anticipated my question. "You want to know why I married him?"

I nodded.

She grimaced. "I don't know why. My curse. I got a talent for picking alkies. My first one was the same way. My second, his thing was drugs, prescription drugs. He was a pharmacist and he was always flying on one of his own prescriptions. And I didn't know it. I learned one evening when I got a call from the cops and the hospital. He O.D.'d while at work, took one too many pills. It was a mess."

"So you divorced him?"

She nodded. "Truth is, he had divorced me a long time before, probably the day we married. First, it was the girls, then the drugs."

"And now your husband . . . ?"

"Bill is drunk on cheap wine when I get home from work every night."

"You want to divorce him?"

She shook her head. "I told you I don't want to, but if I do, it's because he divorced me already, right after we got married, just like my second. He divorced me for his wine. Best thing I can say about Bill is that there aren't any girls in his life. I'm sure of that."

When a client leaves a comment hanging like that, I always oblige and play the straight man. "Why are you sure?"

"Because he's impotent."

Her words did not surprise me. In fact, I had half expected them. What did surprise me was her tone. It was a blend of sarcasm and satisfaction. Betty, to whom sex seemed to be of prime concern, if not a preoccupation, seemed glad that Bill was impotent!

I needed time to think. I repeated her words. "He's impotent."

She nodded. "His penis sort of sums up all the rest of him—flaccid." Her lip had curled when she said that. At that moment Betty did not look attractive at all. Speaking unkindly can do that, even to a beautiful woman.

At the same time, her words and delivery had provided me with an opportunity to achieve some insight into the why of her attitude. "His impotence really makes you mad."

"It disgusts me is what it does. Do you know what it's like to bed down with an impotent man?"

I chuckled. "No, I don't."

Betty didn't chuckle. Instead, she answered shrilly. "You know perfectly well what I mean!"

I nodded. "It was frustrating for you."

"It was a lot more than frustrating. It was humiliating. It made me feel less than a woman."

"When did his impotence start?"

She shrugged. "I'm not sure. Right after we got married. Before marriage, sex was his forte. He was an incredible lover, insatiable. He made me feel like a woman. Do you think this is all due to his drinking?"

I nodded. "It's related certainly. Losing two jobs because of his drinking couldn't make him feel like much of a man. A man who has a profession but can't work is in trouble. Can't feel very good about himself."

"You're right, and it's doing that to me. And I've been living like this for months now. I deserve better."

It was easy now to understand the why of her anger, resentment, and sarcasm. Bill's impotence attacked Betty in the most basic aspect of her person—her womanhood and everything that meant to her. Consciously or unconsciously, by not being able to have sex with Betty, Bill was rejecting her. Whether he saw it that way or not was irrelevant because that is how Betty saw it. The hurt and the anger that she felt prevented her from feeling or expressing any sympathy and told me in the clearest terms that she would indeed be filing for divorce. Betty loved herself too much to do anything else. A corollary thought was that she was probably having an affair.

She had become silent. I repeated her last comment. "You were saying that you deserve better."

"I do. You know, what bothers me about all this is the fact that I married him. I married an impotent man." Again she uttered her pet little ditty, "Sick, eh?"

"I would be more concerned with the fact that you married another alcoholic than that you married a man who became impotent."

She shook her head. "I could live with alcoholism. Alcoholics can be cute. It's the irresponsibility, the womanizing, the lack of interest or caring that come with it that turn me off."

"But, Betty, those are all parts of the disease."

She shrugged.

"You said that alcoholics can be cute."

"And they can be."

I was tempted to ask how, but I knew it would only engender irritation. Instead, I focused on what she was really trying to say. "I gather you don't think alcoholism per se is so bad."

"It doesn't have to be."

This was indeed the adult child of an alcoholic. Denial was her prime defense. I confronted her. "Was your father 'cute'?"

She nodded. "And loving and gentle and giving."

"What did he give you?"

"He gave me him, his time, and he gave me presents too." Her look as she talked became the look of a little girl. "The courts awarded my father weekly visitation rights. Sunday afternoons I saw him. Sunday afternoons were ours. He showered me with affection, bringing me presents every week. Once he went to Canada and brought back a gold maple leaf pin for me. I still wear it. I would spend the whole week making presents for him, drawing pictures, making cut-outs, kid stuff, so that when Sunday came, we could have our own little Christmas. Every Sunday was Christmas because my daddy and I exchanged presents. Looking back now, those were the happiest days of my life." Betty's look was melancholy. "I hate Christmas now. All it does is point out how utterly empty my life is."

I nodded. "The gifts and the attention you got from him made you feel like you were the most important person in the world."

"Or at least in his life." The melancholy look became tearful. She reached for a tissue, dabbed at her eyes. "Then one day we were to go to the beach, and without telling me, without any warning at all, he brought a woman with him. I felt instantly like I had been dropped down into second place."

"How old were you at the time?"

"I was 11."

I nodded, reflected for a couple of seconds, and then I said it. "And from 11 on you've been competing for that first place."

She looked at me surprised, then nodded. A little smile started playing around her mouth. "You're pretty smart to figure that out.

It's true. Ever since then I've wanted to be the best in everything I did. I've wanted to be the focus of attention. And I was, because I was usually the prettiest. But prettiest wasn't enough for me. I was determined to be the smartest. And I was. I graduated first in my high school class and I made Phi Beta Kappa at the university."

She said all that simply, in a detached way, without any bluster, without even a hint of boastfulness. Impressive as were her accomplishments, I was even more impressed by her style. Slowly, subtly, and without my realizing it, she had showed me that there was another side to the shallow, cynical, unthinking, and even unkind Betty. There was a hurt, deprived, wistful little girl there, but a determined one too, who had pursued and achieved excellence without the benefit of support. My heart went out to her.

Our session ended there. At the door she asked me if I thought the session had been informative for me.

I nodded. "You really opened up toward the end about your father and the presents. It was good."

She was standing in front of me, eyes iridescent and glowing. "I'm beginning to feel I can trust you." Her voice was suddenly raspy but its smallness matched the little-girl look I found disturbingly appealing. She must have sensed my reaction because she squeezed my forearm, kissed me on the cheek, and left.

Reflections

This is indeed a woman with a multifaceted personality. Her behavior at the door blended some of the qualities that she had been exhibiting and that continue both to attract me and to make me suspicious. The spontaneity with which she did it was attractive, but I still can't help but feel that there was also a purposeful, manipulative quality to it all. I feel that she is trying to make me another notch on her seduction gun. But why? What's her motive? Is she conscious of it? Could she just be another confused adult child of an alcoholic who is seeing me in therapy because she ran into me in the cafeteria? Such impulsive intrusions and requests for treatment are common among the children of alcoholics. A quick check with Hilda will tell me if she did indeed ask for an appointment. In any case, she's a classic among these adult children, her relationships in disarray, all her husbands addicts, and so on.

Her cruel streak bothers me. And she has one. The positive glee in announcing her husband's impotence tells me she can be castrating, or at least intimidating. To what extent is Bill's impotence a function of her narcissistic demands and of her apparent assurance of her own sexuality? We learned that she is intensely competitive. Was she so with Bill in bed? I wonder. I wonder, too, why she would marry a potential impotent. Was she motivated by some sadistic reason? Another notch on the gun? Or was she again merely feeling the comfortable pull that the adult child of alcoholism feels moving toward the familiar dynamics of alcoholism.

I need to learn more because, while Betty thoroughly enjoys being a woman, there are some quirks in her self-esteem with respect to men. Why this need to seduce?

It is just possible that information about the relationship she had with her mother might be helpful in finding out what Betty really thinks of herself as a person.

I had scheduled Betty for a one o'clock appointment. She was waiting for me when I got back from lunch at 12:45. I had half expected that. Among other things, her exit scene told me that she wanted to get closer.

Some of my queasy feelings about her had returned, and indeed intensified, as I had learned from Hilda that Betty had never spoken to her about making an appointment. She had lied. I wasn't especially surprised. Lying fit with the narcissism, with her background. I learned long ago that many children of alcoholics have a strong tendency to lie, often when they have no reason to. Truth becomes irrelevant when one is reared in a family where denial is a way of life.

Knowing all that still did not mitigate my discomfort or, to be candid, irritation, because now I had to wonder how much of what she had told me was true. Therapy at best is a complex and difficult process. When a client lies, the process becomes impossible. With the children of alcoholics, one of its major functions is to help them understand their denial and the why of it. When they lie, the therapist inadvertently, unknowingly, becomes part of the denial, a part of their whole delusionary system. Under such circumstances, therapy becomes an adventure in fantasy and an exercise in futility. Such were some of my thoughts and feelings when I said, "Hi."

She flashed a radiant smile and preceded me into the office. She wore a short-sleeved blue-green silk dress with a flared skirt. A wide black belt accentuated her small waist. She was holding a square, flat package that had been gift wrapped. Then, with her warm, radiant smile intact, she handed the package to me and said softly, "A very little something I'd like you to have."

Occasionally, at the conclusion of a series of therapy sessions, a client will send me a small gift, or, more commonly, a thank-you note. Gifts after only a few meetings are rare. In light of what I had learned and felt about her, I thought for a split second of not accepting it, realizing as I did that the gift did not signify gratitude so much as it did a need to manipulate and ingratiate. However, I opened it, reminding myself that she was the patient and had asked for help. It was a paper pad bound in black leatherette on which my initials had been imprinted. I read the little card. "Take good notes on me."

She sensed my discomfort, or maybe saw it on my face. "Did I do something wrong?" She added, "It's only a cheap pad."

I shook my head as we took our chairs. "No, not wrong." I let her know what Hilda had told me, explained that I had to know what was true, and finished with, "If you can't be perfectly candid and honest with me, you're going to be wasting your time and mine." As I was talking, I noticed a sad expression come over her face. Her eyes seemed to be moistening.

Looking down, she replied quietly, softly. "It's just what my last counselor told me. I have trouble trusting people and I want to be liked too much."

"Betty," I said evenly, "you told me you'd never had a counselor before."

She didn't respond, just flushed. I very nearly laughed. It was the first good sign. At least she had some kind of a conscience. She looked up. "You may not believe this either, but I don't remember telling you that and I can't imagine why I did."

I told her that I did believe her and her interested, literally rapt expression when I began my explanation about how children of alcoholics perceive the truth changed to one of surprise when she had digested the fact that lying was not an uncommon denominator in their personalities. "You mean there's a reason that I lie."

I shook my head. "It's not cosmic, Betty. You are responsible for your lies." I repeated my explanation.

"I'm just now beginning to realize how much you really understand me," she said in her raspy voice, tinged now with awe.

I smiled. The ingratiation certainly fit with what I understood so far. "Betty, so far you haven't told me very much at all about your mother."

A dark look flitted across her face. "Mother was a bitch."

"How was she a bitch."

"She was mean and spiteful. The court awarded me to her but she never wanted *me* really. She just wanted me to spite my father. He wanted me."

"How do you know that?"

"My father told me he wanted me, and he acted like he did. My mother just used me. Once I heard her say to a friend that the only things my father cared about were 'booze, broads, and Betty.' And she swore he'd never get me." Betty looked away, dabbed at her eyes. "He never did either. He died two nights before I graduated from high school."

"What did he die of?"

"Some kind of hemorrhage."

"How did she treat you?"

"Mean. She never cared how I felt about anything." A hard, bitter tone had crept into her voice. "Her only concern was how I looked. How my hair was done, how my makeup was on, what I was wearing and how everything fit me. She never let me go shopping for clothes by myself, not even for my underwear. She had to approve of everything I wore."

I had a sudden thought. "Betty, did you look like her?"

She nodded her head slowly. "Everybody used to say we could pass for sisters. Same eyes, face, build. We had the same hair too, and even though she kept it bleached, we still looked alike."

"So she passed as a blond."

"Peroxide. I'm sure she thought it made her look younger and it was more attractive to men."

"You talk like it bothered you that she bleached her hair."

Betty spat out her response. "It was so phony."

I was beginning to understand why her view of self and men was so complex.

"Did your mother ever remarry?"

"No. Dozens of boyfriends, not one husband. Even though she used to say she was having too much fun to marry, I think she really wanted to but no one would. I never realized it till now but I guess, except for daddy, no one thought she was the kind you marry." The bitterness in her voice had intensified. "Too much of a crab. I never see her. Christmas, I get a card. Once in a while I get a phone call when she's on one of her weekend trips, from Lake Tahoe or Florida or the Virgin Islands. I think she's trying to impress these guys that she's a good and conscientious mother. Anyway, the calls are always strained. Sad, eh?"

My look told her that yes, it was sad.

"While growing up it was all very crazy because my mother treated me like I was her and at the same time I swear she competed with me. The way she acted with my dates embarrassed and disgusted me."

"What did she do?"

"She flirted. She'd always change and do herself up for them like she was going on the date, not me. And I used to have the feeling she would have gone if she could have. Sick, eh? There was a time when I was in high school that we really did look alike. People used to say all the time that we should go on television and do one of those 'who's the mother, who's the daughter' commercials."

"How did you feel about looking so much like her?"

"I hated it. I hated it because she got all the attention. She was the one everyone fussed over whenever we went anywhere together. It did all kinds of things for her personally, made her feel like she was 20 years younger than she was." Betty paused, then in a heavy tone said slowly, "It did absolutely nothing for me."

"Did it perhaps make you feel older since she was older and she looked so much like you?"

Betty shook her head. "No. But people treated me as if I were older. And I might have acted like I was but the simple truth is that when you're 16, you're still just 16. Your experience is the experience of a child and an adolescent."

I went back to a thought she had expressed before. "What you believe and feel is that your mother was reliving her life through you and at the same time competing with you, not guiding and mothering you."

Betty put on a twisted smile. "For sure, because she certainly was not my role model. Sometimes she tried to act like my girlfriend. You know what she did once?"

"Tell me."

"Once, when I was 18, she actually suggested going on a double date."

"What did you say?"

"I really blew up at her that time. She never suggested it again."

"So you did stand up to her?"

"More and more as I got older." Betty looked away, thoughtfully. "The worst part about my teen years was that I really didn't realize what a bitch she was, what she was doing, how she used me to feed her own ego. You know what I was? I was a big ego trip for my mother. That's all I was. And I didn't understand any of that growing up. I'm just beginning to understand it all now. Sad, eh?"

I nodded. "Sad but understandable. You were living it, you were steeped in it. You didn't, couldn't, have much perspective. The one who knows the least how a war is going is the front-line soldier."

Betty nodded but I sensed she hadn't heard, was immersed in her thoughts. "She robbed me of my teen years. She seemed to know when a dance was coming before I did. She'd take me to buy a gown, and you know what she would do? She would try the gown on! She tried them on first. And in front of the saleswomen she always used the same embarrassing words, with the same sickening sweetness, 'We have the same body, darling.' She never said we're the same size. She had to say, 'We have the same body.' And her other line was, 'Besides, darling, if mother models it for you, you'll know better which one you like.' Actually it didn't matter which one *I* liked because the one we would always end up buying was the one she liked the best. And she really loved trying them on. She'd try on a dozen or more. And, of course, all the salespeople would oooh and ahhh over her and compliment her on her figure. No one even noticed me once she started modeling even though I was the one the dress was for."

Our session ended moments later.

Reflections

Despite her penchant for lying, I find myself beginning to trust Betty. There is little doubt that she is opening up, and truthfully. This opening up, consciously or unconsciously, is motivated by her need to get closer to me, to seduce me. My earlier thoughts on this aspect of her interpersonal style I still believe to be accurate and valid. Whether her intent is a literal seduction or merely to charm and manipulate me to do her bidding I don't know yet.

I am aware, too, that her need to get close may only be a function of the fact that she has entered into transference. If so, it will be interesting to see how long she's in it, how insistent she is to get me to respond to her advances, and to what ends she will go to do so.

The most important information acquired in these last sessions was that she identified strongly with her mother, but is quite oblivious to it. The mother she describes is narcissistic, competitive, demanding, and manipulative, and has a cruel streak. These traits are hers. Her hatred for her mother is very real. How much then can Betty really like herself? What I am just beginning to sense is that her narcissism may be nothing but a defense against a latent but constant and very real feeling of self-loathing, a self-loathing that could well put her into acute depression, and even precipitate suicide. Even as I have this thought, I think it is a bit extreme because I haven't seen any special evidence of this self-hate. Why, then, does the thought persist? Probably because suicide is always a possibility when sense of self is derived from someone whom one hates. Then again, if this surmise about self-hate is correct, Betty should have engaged or should be engaging in self-destructive behavior, or behavior that is socially demeaning or is at least demeaning in one's own eyes. I've seen none and she hasn't discussed anything like that either. Could it be that she's holding back? If she is, then it means that she still is not being completely forthright and does not trust me. (I will need to confront her on this.) That she should feel like this in the confidential and emotionally sheltered climate of counseling makes it even clearer why Betty cannot develop and maintain a long-term close relationship.

She showed up early as she had for the past several appointments. Her hair in tight, tiny ringlets today seemed to glisten more than the usual and contrasted effectively with the snow-white linen suit. The fragrance of her perfume was different, more definite, if not headier; more expensive, I thought.

The look she gave me and her walk as she went to her chair were those of an assured, comfortable woman. Betty felt at home in my office and with me.

Her first words as she relaxed in the recliner confirmed these thoughts. "I've been thinking a lot about our last session and how much I told you. I've never confided in anyone the way I confided in you. I trust you." Her tone as she told me this was low, with a bit of the sexy raspiness I had become used to.

"You trust me?"

"Yes," she said. Her eyes seemed to be emitting little electrical sparks. "I want you to know I respect you."

"Respect," I learned a long time ago, can be a camouflage word. For some it is a way of saying "I love you" without saying it (especially when it is uttered with a rasp). Consciously or unconsciously, I really thought the latter, that Betty was really putting the make on me. It had happened before. Years of doing therapy had provided me with the experience to inure me to the process. What I found disturbing as the session moved on was that I didn't feel particularly experienced or inured to her not-so-latent message. I felt confused, beset as I was by disparate thoughts, some positively lascivious, none of them professional.

Betty knew immediately the effect she was having on me. Before the session was half over, she was giving me little knowing smiles. Even worse, she took control of the session, began asking me about me, my family, my friends, where I lived, even where I socialized and vacationed. And I answered!

Her seduction of me was so effective that the session was nearly over before I realized what I had let happen, that I had let the session dissolve into a waste of time. So complete was my confusion that I didn't have the foggiest notion as to how it all happened.

I, who am positively stuffy about ethics and decorum, had committed a cardinal sin of psychotherapy. Oblivious to my client's needs, I had spent nearly a whole session meeting my own by basking in the adoring gaze of a beautiful woman and responding to a lot of personal and irrelevant questions. And what had happened to all my emotional antennae? I took such pride in always having them up precisely to prevent unhealthy manipulations by a client. Had they been blunted by the perfume? Or was it all simple, primitive lust on my part?

She spoke. "I know I didn't say anything funny. Why the sarcastic grin?"

I didn't respond to her question, but instead asked, "How do you think the session went?"

Her eyes widened, reinforcing both her words and emotion, "Great. Best one we've had!"

"Betty, we've talked only about me."

She nodded happily, "I know. I really feel like I know you now."

With a gentle tone I answered slowly. "The issue, the purpose of these sessions, is for me to get to know you so I can help you understand the why of your problems and . . ."

"But doctor, before you can do that, before I'll let you do that, I have to trust you."

I nodded. "You don't feel you can trust me yet?"

"I trust you more than I ever have any man." The conviction and emphasis in her tone were positively disconcerting.

"Well then!"

"Well then I can't let you into me until I feel I can really trust you."

Her words were so suggestive, so transparent, that I found them embarrassing. She didn't, even though she had to know what she had said. She just gazed at me unblinking, like a competent huntress cat, calculating, waiting, and confident that her wait would pay off.

I didn't feel I was doing therapy anymore but was caught up in some kind of crazy sexual game play, in some ways adolescent, but in some ways so sophisticated it made me very nervous. What made me especially nervous was that Betty felt she had effectively taken control of the session, if not of our relationship. I knew that because in that moment I felt it! I swallowed the unfamiliar lump and watched her gaze and smile at my gulping throat.

When scared, in doubt, or bewildered, I always go to candor. I did so now. "Betty," I said with whatever aplomb I could muster, "right now I feel like your prey, like I'm being stalked."

Her head jerked back. That made me feel better. Chalk one up for candor. "Why do you feel like that?" The innocent tone disturbed me as much as her studied, seductive ploy.

"I feel like that because you've been coming on pretty strong. You say you trust me . . ."

"More than anyone," she cried.

"Good, because we need to be honest with each other."

"I want to be," she said with a sudden wistful look.

I spoke quietly. "Betty, you spent this whole session trying to seduce me."

She didn't answer, just opened her eyes wide again.

"And I fed into it by letting you work at it, by answering your questions about me." I shook my head for emphasis, "And I am simply not the issue or concern of this counseling. You are."

Betty had put on her adoring gaze. My sense of distress, however, had made the flattery go out of it for me. I suddenly found it irritating.

"Doctor," she said with her quiet little rasp, "as usual you're right about everything. If I acted like a scheming vamp, it's only because I found myself attracted to you. I think I'm falling in love with you."

I shook my head and was about to answer when, anticipating my reply, she broke in, her voice suddenly high-pitched and strident. "Please don't tell me what I know I feel."

Her response did not surprise me as it was perfectly consistent with her background and dynamics. What did surprise me was how instantaneous and how acutely honed her premonition was that I was going to reject her advances. Rejection, I had learned quickly, was not something Betty could or would tolerate. It was simply not part of her emotional ken. As she saw it, she was bestowing a rare favor upon me. How could I possibly not accept it? My problem then was to communicate what the real dynamics were here and at the same time let her know that there was no relationship possible for us outside of counseling.

Her eyes seemed to be burning into me as she waited for my response. I cleared my throat. "Betty, if we were to take up together, our counseling relationship would be over."

"But why?"

"Because I couldn't possibly help you."

"But why not?" Her question was more a plaintive wail than a request for an explanation.

"A counselor cannot effectively counsel with someone with whom he's emotionally involved because if he is emotionally involved, he becomes part of the client's dynamics." While I didn't intend it, my tone made the explanation sound a little condescending and not a little pedantic. It was probably my anxiety. In any case, my words were true.

"You don't like me," she said with all the petulance of a nine-year-old child.

Nevertheless, I rewarded it. That's how much I feared that she might terminate counseling. "I like you, Betty. I like you very much."

"Then you don't find me attractive?"

Again I rewarded her, but this time with just a hint of irritation in my voice. "I think you're beautiful, and you know I do."

"Then what's the problem?"

"The problem," I said gently, but firmly, "is not me. It's you."

"What does that mean?" she asked, with no warmth at all.

I leaned forward. "Betty, if we had a sexual relationship, I would be feeding into and compounding all your problems."

"Who said I want to have a sexual relationship with you?" The question was framed in ice. The denial, as conscious as it was unconscious, was, of course, her way of dealing with what she perceived as my rejection.

This was our seventh session and we were at a crossroads. If she didn't admit to the attempted seduction, then she'd probably terminate the counseling. I leaned toward her again, decided to approach her a little more obliquely. "Betty, if we went out together, if our relationship became anything more than a counseling one, I would be reinforcing the low opinion you have of men."

"That one," she cried with verve, "you got wrong, all wrong. I like men."

I nodded. "I'm sure. But relationships with them don't last. And that's why you came to see me, right?"

She nodded, answered in a small voice, "Yes." That "yes" told me she was ready to reassume her role of client.

"I suspect that one of the reasons they don't last is that you don't see them as dependable, reliable, or faithful."

"How do you know I see them like that?"

"I don't know it but I suspect it."

"Why?"

"Because when you meet a man you think you might like, whether you realize it or not, and I'm not sure you always do, your way is to seduce him, if not actually by bedding him down, then by taking control of the relationship."

"How do you know that?"

"Easy. You tried to do that with me. And if you tried to do it here in counseling where you are totally accepted, where you don't have to prove you are lovable, I'd bet anything it's the way you do with most men in whom you're interested."

Betty's shoulders had slumped. She was looking down. "You know I didn't realize at first what I was doing or trying to do with you."

I believed her. "I think you see a man you like or think you might like as a challenge or as someone to play a game with."

She nodded. "It's exactly what my mother told me once. 'It's all a game with them, honey. Just a game. Keep it like that and you'll always be much happier.' " Betty straightened up again and gave a loud cry. "Damn it, I don't want to play games anymore!"

"You want something more?"

Betty sighed, "Yes." She looked at me with the wistful look of a little girl. "Do you think there's any hope for me?"

My grin told her what I thought. So did the facetious tone on which my words rode. "I suspect at age 25 there might be some, yes."

She looked at me sadly. "I'm not so sure. You really don't know me all that well. You really don't know where I've been, what I've been, what I'm capable of."

I looked at her with what I knew was a curious questioning look because these last words were different from a previous session when she talked about how much I understood her. Betty was getting ready to tell me something she thought was significant. "If I don't know you as well as I should, it's probably because you've held back." I looked at her directly.

She held my gaze, nodded.

"Want to tell me?"

"No."

But she would. I waited.

"It happened during my first marriage. Remember, I told you about him, Mr. Boring? Well I was 19. He was 27, going on 97. In addition to all that, we never had any money, or at least I never had any. He doled it out to me."

"Why didn't you get a job?"

"He didn't want me to work. He said he wanted me all to himself. He was crazy jealous."

"So what did you do?" I asked that quietly, softly, and with all the kindness I could muster because I sensed some embarrassment and a lot of pain.

She looked away. "I went to work for this lady."

"Doing what?"

"She called it H and C," she said in a voice that had suddenly taken on a flat, detached quality.

I played her straight man. "H and C?"

"Hostessing and companionship."

I understood. "You were a call girl."

Up to now, even when sad, Betty's face had radiated a healthy, pink glow. Not now. A dark, graylike tone had replaced the glow. It made me think of ominous storm clouds. Suddenly the corners of her mouth started to spasm, and just as she let out a strangled whine, the storm burst. It was like a Niagara, and if nothing else, reflected the veritable reservoir of repressed guilty feelings and conflicts she'd had dammed up for a long time.

I got up and held her. She sobbed for a long time—until the end of the session. When she was done, she looked at me, and with a funny little smile made a weak joke. "Anyway, I got you to hold me."

I smiled.

"I also got mascara all over your shirt front."

I shrugged. "It will wash out."

At the door she looked at me with something akin to adoration. "Think what you like, doctor, but I love you." With that she kissed me on the cheek and left.

Reflections

This was a dramatic and moving session, and one in which Betty learned much and found reward. I know that because I felt very good at its end and my feelings, I've learned, are the best barometer for gauging the productivity and value of a session for a client. A five-star session.

Her words on exiting showed that she had gained some important insight. They had been simple, honest, uttered without any of the seductive rasp to which she had grown accustomed. Indeed, they had been delivered in an asexual tone, in a tone not so much that of woman to man but more as person to person. The ability to talk in this way bodes well for her learning to develop relationships. I'm convinced that her relationships have not endured precisely because her view of the other person is not peerlike but erotic.

Until now I had not been especially hopeful. Now I am. The catharsis she experienced has to be one of the most dramatic and intense that I've observed. But while there is little doubt as to its authenticity and its depth, I know that a catharsis in and of itself does not necessarily precipitate change. Clients not only have to want that change, but they have to effect it. Betty strikes me as a totally able woman with an infinite number of strengths. I'm convinced she can effect it. Whether she really wants to is something else. The change I'm thinking about will require not only a change in how she perceives men but in how she perceives herself, and while Betty's self-perception to date has caused her much pain, it has also brought her a lot of masculine attention.

In subsequent sessions I will need to explore the interplay between her need for this attention and the self-esteem that underlies her apparent narcissism. I suspect that interplay to be the catalyst that precipitated her entry into prostitution.

"And how are you today?"

She nodded, smiled a little too brightly. "O.K., I guess."

I tilted my head to reach her averted gaze. "You're not sure."

She glanced at me. "I've been thinking a lot."

I nodded. "About the time you spent as a call girl?"

Eyes flashing, she replied caustically, "You've talked about how important it is to be candid. Right now what I need is candor."

I looked at her, puzzled.

"Call girl," she said in a tight, ironic voice "is the nicest word you could have used. Right now I prefer some other word for what I did. I checked. A long time ago I checked. Did you know the dictionary has over 30 different synonyms for prostitute? The most descriptive I think are harlot, whore, wanton, and floozie. Those words tell you what I am. What I did. I always thought that the term 'call girl' was about as dishonest as 'hostess and companion.'" Her tone became bitter. "I mean, when you're going down on your knees for perfect strangers you don't exactly fit Amy Vanderbilt's definition of the gracious hostess and companion."

Her unnecessarily graphic allusions to her sexual exploit probably stemmed from an unconscious need to test and shock me. "See how really rotten I am!" At the same time, this vulgarity told me that Betty was very depressed, and remorseful, too, about her escapade into prostitution.

The marginal vulgarities declined as she rattled on at a rapid clip telling me the story of her eight months as a prostitute. And as she did, her face became a mirror reflecting a series of emotions, all negative. I watched fascinated as each one appeared for a moment, then flitted away. Anger was followed by despair, then by resentment, then by fear, then by bewilderment. Bewilderment stayed. "Why? Why did I do it?"

The dismay, the perplexed look, almost made me step out of my role of therapist and into that of a teacher. I knew why, but I also knew that no explanation I could give would have any therapeutic effect. Counseling is not pedagogy. It becomes therapeutic and effects

meaningful changes when the client is emotionally ready to understand and accept the why. She just wasn't ready. I smiled reassuringly.
"We'll learn why, I'm sure. Some of that why may be in something
you told me that you heard your mother say."

"What?"

"It had to do with your father and the only things he cared about."

Betty nodded. "Booze, broads, and Betty."

"What I find interesting is that the line has stayed with you all
these years. That line continues to have a lot of meaning for you."

"She was talking about my father. And I loved him."

"I know that. But that's not what's important."

"What's important?"

"Was there any truth to it?"

Betty's whole body jerked back as if I had hit her. "Why, what
do you mean?"

I found it hard to say what I had to but I had to guide her into
the basic realization. "You told me your father was alcoholic and that
he was the only person who ever loved you."

She nodded and suddenly sat up, assuming a tense, rigid position
as if she knew she was going to have to steel herself against my words.
I sighed unhappily and asked the question. "Is the middle part of your
mother's little ditty true too?"

Betty smirked. "You mean about broads?"

"About broads."

She looked away. "He was a man. Yes, I guess he liked women."

Resistance to acknowledging the question is a sure sign that the
client has walled up the answer to keep it from conscious awareness.
How thick or thin that wall was depended on how painful it was to
admit and answer the question. I had no interest in exacerbating that
pain. When the situation gets tense, I try to proceed slowly, gently.
Sometimes I inject a little humor. "Nothing you said to me before
suggested that he was gay."

She chuckled. "Daddy was not that."

The positive verve in her reply told me that the wall was thinner
than it was thick. "You said that you really knew about your father
and his women friends."

She didn't answer.

"Painful to talk about it, isn't it?"

She nodded. "Is it necessary?"

"It's necessary. You told me how your father brought a woman
with him when you and he were going to go swimming."

"Yeah. I remember her vividly. I was eight years old and skinny.
She was bosomy—a bosomy, blond broad."

Betty, I observed, had her mother's taste for alliteration.

"You didn't like her?"

"No. But then I didn't like any of them."

"There were others then?"

She literally snapped her answer. "Of course there were others!"

"How many others?"

"God, who can remember?"

"And he brought them around every Sunday?"

"He used to leave them in the car while he picked me up and then I sat in the back seat. The back seat, never in the front seat! I was his daughter, and I always took a back seat to his floozies."

Floozies, I recalled, was one of the terms she felt best expressed what she herself had been.

"They all seemed to come from the same mold. They all looked alike, talked alike, and acted alike. They were all so stupid. They reminded me of a bunch of Barbie dolls. And they were all after him. Even as a child I could see that. By the time I got to my teens I found them nauseating."

"You told me once that you competed with them."

"Yes, I did."

"It was basically unfair competition wasn't it, Betty?"

"Of course! I was a skinny little kid . . ."

"And they were blond, bosomy broads, these companions of your father." I thought I was being sensitive and delicate in my choice of words, but even as I said it, I realized that this was the term used by her employer. Ironically, it had a much desired effect.

"Companions, shit! They were whores!"

"Is that anger talking or do you know they were that?"

"They never were around long. I never saw any of them more than a few times. What else could they have been?"

"What I think you mean is that they were his bed mates."

"Whore. Bed mate. Same thing. Neither one lasts very long, and none of them did either."

"Your father never had a long relationship with any of them?"

"Whores don't have relationships."

I waited a moment, hoping she would hear and feel the profound meaning of her own words. She didn't. I repeated them ever so slowly, "Whores don't have relationships."

She didn't pick up on my reiteration. I leaned back, thinking. There was little doubt that Betty had in some measure identified with one or more or with the collection of these women. But with what had she identified? "Tell me," I said slowly, talking out a thought I was having, "did you like how they looked?"

Betty's look was both quizzical and surprised. "Why do you ask me that?"

"Well, you were a little kid. They were adult women. They were close to your father. Did you think they were pretty, some of them!"

She sighed. "Yes."

"And you wanted to look like them?"

"Yes."

She grinned wryly. "When I was about 12, I remember putting all kinds of things in my bra."

I nodded. "That figures."

"What about the hair? You said a couple of times they were blonds."

"Yeah, they were." She looked away, spoke with embarrassment, "One Saturday night I bleached my hair."

"To look attractive for your father?"

"I guess."

"What was his reaction?"

"He was very polite. He said he liked it. I don't know if he really did. What bothered me most was the reaction of the bitch in the front seat. She laughed so hard she made my father laugh. Then she spent the whole day telling me I shouldn't be unhappy about how I looked because it would offend God." She glared. "Imagine that sanctimonious hypocritical whore had the audacity to talk to me about God!" Betty paused, was quiet for a few moments.

Her anger about something that had happened over half of her lifetime ago was still pretty strong. That told me that not only had the hurt been considerable but also that, consciously or unconsciously, she might be holding back something. I was about to break the silence, to probe and see if my surmise was correct. I thought better of it and just waited. The wait proved rewarding.

"You know what really bothered me about that woman?"

"What?"

"She had dark roots. She wasn't even a real blond herself."

"Did you tell her?"

"No. I was only a little kid. Little kids don't tell grown-up strangers that they're hypocrites. Anyway, I hate blonds and hypocrites."

What is transparently apparent to the therapist is often hidden, or at best nebulous, to the client. I spoke slowly. "What you're saying, Betty, is that you hate your mother."

She had been about to say something. My comment closed her open mouth, made her jaw go slack as the obvious struck. She gave a loud sigh. "Of course. I was a kid and so confused. All I knew was the kind of hair to which he was attracted."

"And unlike your mother, your hair was not blond."

"Wrong hair, wrong father, wrong mother."

The look on her face as she spoke those words was totally bleak and one of deep hurt. Right then I felt as though I was on her emotional wavelength, sensed that we had reached an empathic moment. I uttered the words I knew she was feeling. "Here you were, a little bewildered girl budding into womanhood with no support from anyone. Your own mother was a competitor. Then you had to compete with a whole assortment of women for the love and attention you should have had just because you were his daughter, just because you were a human being."

Betty burst into tears. "Whose fault? Whose fault was it? My father's? My mother's? Mine?"

I stood up, crouched next to her chair, and spoke softly. "Finding fault will get you nothing. Not reason, not explanation, not even satisfaction. You lived in the situation in which you lived. Your father was diseased with alcohol, your mother with narcissism."

She stopped crying. "Not fair."

I nodded. "You're right. It isn't."

"I deserved better."

"For sure, but what you didn't get psychologically you did get intellectually, physically. Some people get nothing." Those words, intended to be supportive and uplifting, smacked a little of the "be grateful for what you got, kid," or, if not sanctimonious, they were at least condescending. Fortunately, Betty looked as though she had not even heard me, as though her mind were on another thought.

"You know, on that whole subject of blonds there's something I didn't tell you."

"You want to now?"

"Not really."

"Embarrasses you?"

She nodded. "More than that, I'm just beginning to realize how much I sought to be everything that I hated. Just starting to realize how sick I can be." Then, looking away, she said, "I wore a wig for a while."

"A blond wig?"

She nodded slowly.

"And you figure that that was sick because it means that you wanted to be like your mother or your father's blond friends?"

"Yeah. God, I was so confused. I still am. Why would I want to be like her, like them, when I hated them all so?"

"You wanted to be like your mother, probably are like her somewhat, precisely because when you were a little kid you didn't see too many alternatives. Kids want to be people. They want to develop a personality. Have to. The alternative is madness."

"So rather than go nuts, I became like my mother. Are you saying that?"

"Yes, I guess I am."

Betty laughed. "Here I am today talking to a shrink because as a kid I identified with my mother rather than go crazy. That, dear doctor, is what's crazy."

I nodded. "It is, but I think it's true."

"I haven't told you everything about the wig."

"So," I chuckled, "tell me."

"It was what I wore when I did my little H and C routine."

My head jerked slightly in surprise.

She caught the surprise. "I told you how sick I can be."

What she had told me should have come as no surprise at all. I should have known; indeed, I should have anticipated it. Wearing a wig as an H and C was perfectly consistent with the dynamics of the case, with her feelings about herself, her father, and her mother. "Tell me, why do you think you wore it as an H and C? I take it, it was only in those circumstances that you wore it?"

She nodded. "Yeah, I never wore it before or since. Why did I wear it playing hooker? I wore it because it was a pretty good disguise."

"You wore it because you didn't want to be recognized."

"Of course I didn't want to be recognized. I mean, I wasn't exactly proud of it. And I can tell you don't believe my reason."

"I believe you. I believe you believe what you're saying."

"But it isn't the real reason for you, is it? Well damn it. I was the hooker. I was the whore. I know what I did and I know why." She said all that in a high-pitched strident voice, but somehow it lacked conviction. She sounded a little as though she were trying to convince herself as much as me.

"I also did it for money and because I was lonely and because my husband was a complete bore."

I nodded. "I wouldn't dispute any of those reasons. They may be valid."

"But?" She asked with a grimace.

I leaned forward as I do whenever I want to communicate my earnestness. "Betty, what you told me is that your father liked blonds. And if I read you right, he went out only with blonds. And you, Betty, adored this father from whom you never got enough love and attention. You hated your mother with whom you identified, and she was a blond via hydrogen peroxide. From what I gather, you learned that if blonds don't have more fun, they do get a lot more attention. Look at your mother. Bleached blond! And your father married her! So you bleached your hair, just like your mother."

Betty gave me a very impatient look. "What's your point, doctor, that I always wanted to be a blond?"

I nodded. "That, but right now we're discussing you're wearing of a blond wig and why you did."

She looked at me, eyes suddenly very soft. "Why do you find it so hard to say what I was?"

"What?"

"Hooker, whore, prostitute, take your pick."

She *had* picked it up. I was embarrassed but spoke my feelings. "I guess it's because I don't see you as one and because I know you are so very much more."

She jumped up and gave me a quick, hard kiss on the mouth. "Doctor, sometimes I think *you're* seducing *me*."

I laughed, "Betty, that problem you don't need. Now back to what I was saying." I paused, thought for a second. Did I want to? More important, was she ready? I did it. "Your father was attracted to blonds. When you worked as a hooker, you portrayed yourself as a blond." I lowered my voice. "Does that mean anything to you?"

She nodded slowly, spoke in a small voice, "It's transparent. I sought to be my father's whore."

"Yes. And there's more. Like it or not, you identified a lot with your mother whom you see in the same light as your father's women friends."

"A whore?"

"If you like, yes. Identified means you saw yourself as her."

"I felt that I was a whore like her?"

"Yes, and remember that you said that you weren't exactly proud of being a whore." (She was right. I didn't like saying it.) "The truth was that you were ashamed of it, probably repulsed by it. But you did it, and you did it to fulfill the vilest expectations you had of yourself. What you were doing was confirming what and who you understood you were. At the same time, and crazy and perverted as it may sound, a major reason you were a whore was to punish an alcoholic father who never gave you much love or attention and a narcissistic mother who gave you less."

Throughout my little analysis, Betty had maintained a look I could best characterize as one of polite disbelief. "I was a whore because I wanted to punish my parents?" The incredulity in her tone confirmed my view of the expression on her face.

I nodded. "Yes, but more than that, it was basically because you saw yourself as a whore."

"God, I'm even sicker than I thought."

I shook my head, spoke seriously and with all the conviction I could muster. "Not so much sick as unique. You're different, Betty."

"I sure am," she exclaimed. "Phi Beta Kappa and a whore."

"You're Phi Beta Kappa, true," I shot back, "but you're a whore only if you insist on seeing yourself as one."

She didn't reply for several moments, then looked up. "It's true. I don't think too much of myself do I?"

"No," I said heavily, "you don't."

"So what do I do?"

The clock told me that our time was up. "Right now, not too much. If you want, we'll see each other again next week."

"I want. Can you make it this week? Can I see you twice a week?"

I nodded.

Reflections

I wonder if my analysis did not come a little too early. I said a lot. Was she emotionally ready to digest it all? Our next session will tell.

The pain and embarrassment she went through talking about the wig inform me that she trusts me. The spontaneity with which she kissed me confirms it.

She's still got a crush on me. Those little adoring glances, while only sporadic now, are still occurring. Her control in this regard, however, seems to be getting better. I'm sure she will feel the need to try to seduce me again. The try will probably be couched in what she perceives to be a perfectly respectable mode. We will see.

Epilogue

My feeling that Betty still harbored erotic feelings about me proved correct. Toward the end of a subsequent session, she told me that she had filed for divorce and was feeling especially blue and lonely. Then, with her eyes riveted on mine, she rasped out her invitation, "I know you have evening appointments on Thursday night. Could you stop by for a drink afterward? I'd really appreciate it."

I meet with only a few select clients on Thursday nights. Very few people knew that. Betty knew. I wasn't especially surprised. Clients in transference expend a lot of energy learning about their therapist. I replied kindly but firmly, "Honestly now, did you think I'd say yes?"

She smiled ruefully. "I guess not." Then, still smiling, she spoke the words that told me her perception of men was getting better. "There really are guys like you, aren't there?"

I chuckled. "I suspect there are a lot of guys like me."

Then, wistfully, she asked me the core question, "Do you really think I can be a one-man woman?"

"Yes, because I sense you are beginning to realize that you don't have to seduce to relate."

I continue to see Betty on a biweekly basis and have done so now for six months. Our principal topics have been two: Betty; and Betty in relation to men.

What she has learned was what I had long suspected she would. Beneath her veneer of sophistication and narcissism beats the heart of a fearful and lonely little girl. That little girl is still in Betty and only now is suffering all the growing pains of normal children. But she is growing up, albeit slowly.

Her constant feelings of fear and aloneness were the prime reasons she had entered marital relationships. Betty discovered that she had never married for love. Indeed, she's still not sure what it is. She discovered, for example, that she's never found any joy in giving or in receiving. Both acts, she felt, had to do with game playing, with the victor getting the loser into bed. It was for that reason that she constantly gave men little presents—to seduce them. It was for that reason, too, that she eyed every gift to her with acute suspicion. Right now she's searching to learn to give without ulterior motive and just because she wants to. She's begun giving again, so far only to women friends at work but she finds she "gets a kick out of it." Her response to gifts from them has been comparable. At the same time, we are both aware that the truer test, the harder learning, will be with men because of the sexual component. "I'm sorry, doctor," she cried out recently, "that's how I see them—as sexual objects."

"Do you see me like that?"

The surprise on her face matched the tone in her voice. "No, I don't."

"You did once though, didn't you?"

"Yes. My god, there is hope."

I nodded. "There's hope."

5

THE
WENTWORTH
FAMILY

"Bodies Don't Lie."

Albert Wentworth is not much to look at. In his mid-30s, sandy-haired, brown-eyed, and narrow-shouldered, he is no more than five feet five inches tall and weighs less than 140 pounds. Unfortunately, this nondescript physique is matched by a face that is also something less than attractive. His nose is small but bulb-shaped, his lips are pencil-line thin, and his small, darting eyes make one think of a scared crow.

As we exchanged greetings and simple chit-chat, I realized that I had known him for over ten years. We had first met at a Parent's Night at the junior high school. He was my son's English teacher. Since that first meeting, we had met a couple of times at parties.

He expelled a long baleful sigh and spoke, "You probably know why I'm here."

I shook my head. "No, Al," I said, "I don't. Why should I know?"

"Well, it's all over town. I can tell the way people look at me. Everybody knows."

Unfortunate but true, clients tend to think that their problems are the focal point of public attention. I spoke cheerfully. "O.K. tell me what everybody knows so I can know too."

"We're having problems. Fifteen years now and we're having problems."

"You're talking about you and your wife, Jill?"

He nodded miserably.

I wasn't surprised. A stranger, asked to pair up married couples, would never choose Jill to go with Al. She was as beautiful as he was not. She was also as effervescent in disposition as he was morose. Like many, I'd overheard the snide and petty references to beauty and the beast. Even though I didn't like it about myself, I too was petty enough to wonder why and how they had come to marry. "Why do you believe everybody knows you're having problems in your marriage?"

"Why? Why? because whenever we go to a party now, she gets drunk and flirts with all the guys. It's embarrassing. Like I say, everybody has to know."

I didn't know, but then again I wasn't surprised as I'm never up on town gossip, "How long has she been doing that?"

He shook his head dismally. "Long time, a year, two. I'm not sure."

"Does she get drunk at home?"

Again he shook his head. "I don't know. I don't think so." Then he cried out, "I love my wife!"

Non sequiturs are not uncommon at initial sessions. They reflect the anxiety and stress clients feel. I found this one, however, a little more curious than most. He claimed to love his wife and yet seemed ignorant of some of her basic habits at home. I leaned back. "Al, why don't you fill me in about yourself and Jill."

They both came from a fair-sized city in southern New Hampshire, he said. Al's father had owned an insurance and real estate business. An only child, Al had been educated at Exeter and Dartmouth. "Jill never went to college. Her folks were poor French Canadians. She's got seven brothers and sisters." His tone, which blended satisfaction with condescension, told me the marriage had had problems from the start.

"Tell me, Al, did anybody in Jill's family have a drinking problem?"

He nodded hard. "Her father. I won't say he was exactly the town drunk but everybody in town knew Rene Bombard drank too much. He was unreliable, couldn't keep a job. That's why his family was so poor. They were so poor that they were one of the families that received food and charity from the church." His tone, I noticed, continued to meld satisfaction with condescension.

"What about drink in your family?"

Al shook his head slowly. "My father drank hardly at all. His favorite line was, 'A man should be in control always.' He always was."

"What about your mother?"

He looked away. "Well, she wasn't alcoholic, if that's what you want to know."

The defensiveness of the response was a cue that, at the very least, Al had been bothered about his mother's drinking and/or harbored some denial about it.

"She drank?"

"Yeah, she did." He sounded embarrassed.

"Sometimes a little too much?"

He shot me an impatient look. "Doctor, what the hell does this have to do with my problem now?"

I replied quickly. "Probably a lot. I've learned that your wife came from an alcoholic family and I'm learning that you may have also."

Albert bellowed his response. "Mine was not an alcoholic family."

That bellow convinced me that this was a topic that I needed to explore further. But not now. We didn't know each other well enough yet. Further questioning could precipitate a quick termination. "O.K., your family wasn't alcoholic. Jill's was."

"Very much so. She's got two brothers who are. One's in the hospital right now."

"Tell me, Al, why did you marry Jill?" Even though I thought I knew the answer, I wanted to hear his response. It could tell me a lot about his dynamics, particularly how he perceived the relationship.

After a few moments in which he looked properly thoughtful, Al replied, "I married her because I loved her."

I nodded. "I'm sure of that."

Still looking pensive, he said, "And I married her because she needed me. I've never told this to anyone but I felt sorry for her, sorry for the incredible poverty she lived in, sorry for the alcoholic father."

"You wanted to rescue her from her father and the squalor?"

He grinned. "Something like that, yeah."

I believed that he believed everything he told me. That he saw himself in part as a kind of Prince Charming did not surprise me, as it provided him with a nice justification to view Jill as a kind of Cinderella. What Al was telling me, then, was that when he married Jill, he did her a big favor. But Al was telling me far more, because he did not even mention her beauty. Was he denying that she was beautiful? If so, this could well be the source of at least some of their problems. Such a level of denial would be perfectly consistent with one brought up with alcoholic dynamics. At the moment, the apparent denial reinforced my notion that one parent at least, probably his mother, was alcoholic.

"You know, doctor, this whole thing with Jill has really got me stymied, and it's got me stymied because I can't count on her like I used to. I mean, she's drunk a good portion of the time."

I kept my face impassive on that bit of news. He was quite unaware that he had already told me that he either didn't know or didn't think that she drank at home. Like non sequiturs, conflicting statements at initial therapy sessions are not uncommon, and like them too, reflect emotional confusion. However, I always find the conflicting statement more disconcerting with the adult children of alcoholics because often it reflects one of the common denominators in their personality, namely, a cavalier lack of concern for the truth. I addressed his comment. "What do you have to count on her for?"

His eyes grew wide as he exclaimed. "Why the kids. The kids. She's supposed to be a mother."

He told me that they had two children, a boy and a girl, 13 and 14, respectively. "I think Jill's drinking is affecting Bill a lot more than it is Penny. Penny's like me, a doer, into a lot of different activities but laid back when it comes to people. Billy's more like his mother, always talking, laughing, and joking with people."

"What's the matter with that?" I asked.

Al shook his head. "Nothing. Except now he's not talking much and he never laughs anymore. I'm sure it's because of what he sees."

"What does he see?"

"A mother who is a drunk."

I decided to confront. "Al, at one point you told me you didn't know if she drank at home and now you're telling me your son sees Jill drunk. Help me understand."

Al looked confused for a moment, but only a moment. The confusion evaporated and was replaced by his more familiar expression of gloom. "Doctor, you have to understand that we're all very embarrassed by this. Takes a while to admit and talk about it. In fact, you're the first person I've talked to about it."

I found his use of the word "we" amusing. At the same time, it helped me to believe the explanation. His response to my next question confirmed that belief. "Do you talk about it with your children?"

"God no!"

What I was learning fast was that Albert lived with a lot of denial, probably learned in childhood, and that he was teaching his children to do the same. This is a classic method in the alcoholic family.

"What good would it do to talk to them? They're only kids."

I felt impatience rising, but kept it off my face and out of my voice. "If Jill is drinking, I'm sure you're right in your assumption that your kids see it. Not discussing it with them is telling them that's it's O.K. to live in a home and a world that's not true or real."

Al's response made me think he wasn't attuned to what I was saying. His response was, "Poor kids."

"Al," I said (despite my awareness and control the impatience had crept into my voice), "the poor kids don't have to be abandoned by both parents."

"I'm not abandoning them!"

"You just said that you don't talk to them about what you're presenting to me as the major problem in your family."

"Not talking to them is not abandoning them!" he insisted in a harsh tone.

Dueling with a client can be profitable sometimes. This, however, was not one of those times. He was very threatened by the idea that he had abandoned or was emotionally distant from his children. That told me his denial on this topic was very weak. Al, I concluded, was not close or comfortable with either wife or children. Whatever his dynamics, his present gloominess was very apparent and very real. His next words told me that he was very much attuned to my train of thought.

"It didn't used to be like it is now. We were all very much closer."

"Family's not close like it used to be?"

"No, it isn't," he replied sadly.

I fed into what I knew he was thinking. "She's just not a mother anymore."

He nodded. "Booze has got to her. She's got no interest in the family, in the kids, in me. Mothers just shouldn't drink."

The last line fueled my sense that he was not talking about Jill only. I repeated it. "Mother's shouldn't drink."

"No. They're just too important. Alcoholic mothers corrupt the spiritual and moral fabric of a family. They make for divorce. Very depressing."

Despite the bleak words, Al was not emitting much emotion. There was a detachment and an objectivity in his voice that made me think he was not as depressed about the current state of affairs at home as he liked to indicate. "Are you thinking of divorcing Jill?"

"God no! How could I possibly do that? It would rock us. Who would take care of the kids? She can't or won't by herself and I have to work. I'm with Bancroft, you know. Supposed to be part-time but

I find myself spending as much time there as I do at school."

Bancroft was a large real estate firm in town. "So you're not home a lot?"

He nodded. "On a teacher's salary I have to work on the side if I'm going to support my family." His tone was resigned but there was more than a hint of pride in it, too.

"Al, clear this up for me. Just how drunk does Jill get at home?"

"I just said I work a lot. I'm not really sure."

"At dinner time, for example, is she under the weather?"

He shook his head, "Not noticeably, but again I'm not home for supper a lot. It's just too good a time to show houses."

"Well, how do you know she's drunk all the time?"

"Because the liquor cabinet's always empty. I can't seem to keep it full like I used to."

"You keep it full?" I tried to keep any hint of incredulity out of my voice. I was not completely successful.

He nodded. "Have to. You can't have people visit and not offer them a drink. My father used to say that a well-stocked liquor cabinet is the best sign of a gracious host."

I didn't even try to keep the irony out of my voice. "And if you do not keep a well-stocked cabinet, you are not gracious, eh?"

Al didn't respond to the irony, not in words or by expression, such was the extent of his denial of what he was saying here and doing at home.

"So she empties the liquor cabinet, which you keep restocking?"

"Yeah."

"You're sure it's she who's drinking it and not the kids?"

"Positive. She's not gotten to the point where she drinks secretly like a lot of women closet drinkers. She's open enough about it. She's usually drinking when I get home at night."

"Is she drunk?"

He shrugged. "I can't tell."

He was giving me information but there was more than a little resistance too, as he was volunteering little. Was he conflicted about being disloyal? Was it a lack of trust in me? Or was it that he just didn't feel he knew? I probed. "Well, does she slur her words?"

He shook his head. "She holds her liquor pretty well still."

"What do you mean by still?"

"Well, after a while an alcoholic's tolerance disappears. Everybody knows that."

No, not everybody knows that. Al knew that. I didn't react to the statement but instead focused on his need to see his wife as alcoholic. "Al, how often do you stock the cabinet?"

He shrugged. "Couple of times a month."

"With how much liquor?"

"Some gin, a little scotch, maybe some rye. I buy a variety."

"This is for guests, too?"

"Yes."

The whole tenor of the conversation gave me the impression that the amount purchased was not a stupendous amount.

"I'm wondering if Jill is really alcoholic."

"Oh she is, believe me!"

I responded patiently. "So far Al the only definitive bit of information you've given me is that she drinks too much at parties."

"And flirts with every guy there!"

Right then I knew that Jill's flirting bothered him a lot more than her drinking, which I was not sure was alcoholic. There was only one way to determine that. I told him. "Al, I need to see Jill if I'm going to be of any help."

"What if she won't come?" he asked.

I told him that if she didn't, I couldn't be of much help, and that the marriage was indeed in trouble. I didn't tell him that if she refused to come, it might also be an indication that she was alcoholic. Alcoholics are very resistant to having their schedules and their lives disrupted.

We decided not to make another appointment until I heard from him or Jill.

Reflections

My sense is that the problems with this marriage stem from the perception that Jill and Al had of each other when they married. My surmises are that she saw him as a security blanket and he saw her as a status symbol. These surmises are premised not only on what he did and didn't tell me, especially with respect to her beauty, but on two common denominators found in the personalities of children of alcoholics—a neuroticlike need for security and a neuroticlike need for love.

The unpredictable, untrusting climate of the alcoholic home invariably promotes insecurity in the children. Their response to such unpredictability is invariably an acute concern for security. If you add poverty, it becomes an obsession. My sense is that it became so for Jill.

Al's socioeconomic status alleviated, or at least ameliorated, her obsession. She, in turn, met his preoccupation for love. His comments on a mother's role, and especially about a mother's drinking, fed my impression that his own mother was probably alcoholic. What we know is that alcoholic mothers have difficulty with giving and accepting love, and that their children are invariably in acute need of it. Al's presumed deprivation and lack of knowledge about it, together with his unfortunate physical appearance, probably convinced him that he would never have love or, at the least, made him anxious about the probability of his entering and developing a relationship from which he could get love.

The satisfaction and condescension in Al's tone convince me that those two emotions play a part in how he perceives and interacts with Jill. Both feelings can only contribute to the feelings of low self-esteem that Jill must have despite her beauty. And ironically, that apparent beauty is probably what feeds Al's self-esteem. With Jill on his arm, he is doubtless able to see himself as having much more status and this enables him to function with others far more effectively. When Jill flirts at parties, his self-esteem must suffer excruciatingly. In a real sense, she is the cornerstone of his self-esteem. This is why I believe he is far more disturbed about her flirting than he is about her drinking. It is why he came to see me. And if she is flirting at parties, it tells us much about what she thinks of Al, herself, and the viability of her marriage.

I hope she calls me.

The ringing of the telephone was long, loud, and insistent, a veritable assault on my drowsy senses. As I fumbled for the phone in the dark, I stubbed my toe and cursed. For many years now I have debated about having a phone installed near my bed. Finally, I always decide against it because I hate to be startled into wakefulness. I decided forthwith to have it put in. Being startled, I decided, had to be preferable to a stubbed toe. Still in the dark, I picked up. My hello, while not angry, was not exactly receptive either.

"Doctor Perez, this is Jill Wentworth."

"Hi, Jill."

"I'm sorry to bother you at such a late hour."

"It's O.K.," I said, switching on the light. I glanced at the clock and winced. "What's up?"

"I just wanted to let you know that I do want to see you with Al. He just came in and told me that you asked to see me."

With whatever patience and gentleness I could muster at 12:45 a.m., I told her to call my office and tell my secretary that I'd like to schedule her for the first available hour.

Still more drowsy than awake, I realized that Jill's call was among the few I had ever received at such a crazy hour. "I'm probably lucky."

I yawned as I felt my way back into bed. Was she drunk? I doubted that. Her words had not been slurred. Bad judgment? Maybe. One thing for sure, Al had to be the hardest working of real estate salesmen—or he didn't like talking to his wife at sane hours. Drifting back to sleep, I realized that I was glad that she had called, stubbed toe and all.

Jill and Al were in the waiting room when I opened my office door. I hadn't seen Jill in many months. Her dress, a white and blue floral print, contrasted attractively with short jet black hair worn in a layered windblown style. Jill is at most five feet two but she is one of those people who looks taller. Maybe it's because she walks so erectly. She came toward me and flashed a broad smile, "Hi, doctor."

I returned her greeting, nodded to Al, and led them in. I waved in no special direction. "Take a seat." Al chose the right side of the two-seater couch. Jill took a step toward the left side then veered to my right into one of the two recliners. I chose the other one.

"Let me begin by apologizing again for calling you so late. I was in the middle of a book when Al came in and told me you wanted to see me. I just didn't realize how late it was."

"You didn't realize because you'd been drinking. That's why you didn't realize. Let's face it. That's why we're here. You drink too much."

Jill gave him a cold, impassive look, turned her pale-blue eyes toward me. "I had two gin and tonics all night. My friend has got a thing about my drinking. He insists on calling me an alcoholic."

Al responded through clenched teeth. "You got polluted at the last three parties."

His wife smirked a little and then nodded. "I was feeling pretty good, that's true, and that's all that's true."

Al leaned forward and cried out, "Why don't you tell him how you were making out with every guy there!"

The light makeup did not hide the pink spread of embarrassment. It started at her throat, spread quickly across her cheeks. She looked down and spoke in a small controlled voice. "I didn't make out with every guy there."

Al literally spat out his reply, "I saw you kissing Stevens."

She looked at me with a sad little smile. "And that's all I did. I kissed him on the cheek."

I grinned at her. "Why?"

She shrugged. "Because he said something nice to me." She looked at her husband sarcastically, then turned to me. "That doesn't happen too often in my life."

Al's reply was acrimonious and instant. "Maybe I don't say nice things because you don't do too much that's nice."

The only effect that pettiness and vitriol ever have on me is to nauseate me. That was how I was feeling now. I confronted them and my feelings. "This kind of talk makes me feel very uncomfortable," I said in a flat, detached voice.

Jill nodded. "I know the feeling. I've got it all the time."

"You bicker like this a lot?" I asked, looking from one to the other.

Al expelled a loud sigh. "It's either bicker or no talk."

There was a moment's lull. Both looked at me expectantly. I asked the obvious. "And how long has it been like this?"

Jill's voice was heavy and gloomy. "A long time."

"Why do you think it's like that, Jill, bicker and no talk?"

She looked at me, her eyes suddenly moist. "I feel trapped," she said in a choked voice.

Al rolled his eyes to the ceiling. "Now comes the dramatics."

"Why do you feel trapped?"

"He's stifling."

"What she means is that I don't want her to work."

"He doesn't want me to do anything. He's incredible," she cried. "He treats me like we were living in the 19th century."

"What she's trying to say is that I want her to act like a wife and a mother and she doesn't want to be either."

"That's not fair, and you know it. I'm close to my kids. They don't even know you."

She turned to me. "I want to mother. I always did. I like it. But I want to work. I want to get a job. God, I just want to feel like I'm useful."

Al mimicked her. "I want. I want. I want. What about what the family wants?"

She glared at him. "Both kids want me to work and you know it. You're the one who doesn't want me to. And we both know why."

"Why?" I asked.

"Because he's insanely jealous, that's why. He thinks somebody's going to steal me away from him."

Al, slumped in his chair, didn't answer.

Jill shook her head. "It's all too bad."

Al cleared his throat. "Well, Christ, when you sidle up and flirt with guys at parties all you do is make me feel like I'm right, absolutely right." He paused, adding slowly and with conviction, "Wives who are mothers have a responsibility to keep the home."

Jill looked at me. "Honest now, do you know anybody else who talks like that? 'Mothers have a responsibility to keep the home!'."

I don't answer rhetorical questions but I suspect that my look told her that, no, I didn't know anybody who speaks like that. I knew what she meant when she talked about the 19th century. The line was right out of it.

"You know why my friend talks like that?" she asked. The tone this time was not rhetorical but angry and demanding. I should have moved the discussion in another direction. I didn't. Instead I turned to him, toned my question facetiously, "Why, Al?"

He reddened, "Let her tell you since she's burning to."

I was acutely uncomfortable now, but since I didn't know what else to do, I turned to her with a questioning look.

She looked at her husband while she said, "His mother spent the last years of her life in and out of a sanitorium for alcoholics."

I have always disliked unearthing family skeletons, especially when the person to whom the skeleton belongs is not ready to do the un-earthing. The moment was an awful one, because I could feel Jill's embarrassment in saying the words and having Al hearing them. I could have kicked myself for letting it happen. Predictably, Al's hostility was exacerbated.

From his slumped position, he snapped his displeasure. "You had to tell him, didn't you?"

"I told him because you wouldn't and I'm tired of living a lie."

"What does that mean?" he asked, sitting up.

"Just that. We're living a lie. In fact, we are living lies, you and I."

Al's face had become very red, "What the hell are you talking about?" he cried.

Jill leaned forward in her chair, directed her words toward me. "Our kids never knew her, and whenever he talks about her, he talks about her as if, when she died, some kind of mold for mothers was broken."

"What about your father?" I asked her. "Do they believe the same about him?"

Her eyebrows raised. "So, you told the doctor about my father?"

"Yes."

She looked at him with a knowing little smile. "How interesting! Tell us, Al, do the kids know about him?"

"If they do, they didn't hear it from me," he said.

She looked at me. "I don't think they know."

There was a moment's lull, then Al spoke, a hint of a whine in his voice. "I just don't think it's right for kids to hear that their grand-parents were alcoholics."

"That man," she said, tilting her head with positive disgust, "can-not admit to anything."

"Damn it, Jill, what good does it do for them to hear that they come from diseased stock?"

She glared at him. "I am sick and tired of being referred to like I am a piece of livestock."

"I'm sorry. I know you don't like that expression but I was talking about me too. It's just a figure of speech."

"Figure of speech, crap!" she cried. "I swear, you do think of yourself as some kind of a sick bull. Well, you had better get this straight, my friend, once and for all. I am not a sick cow. Anyway," she said suddenly, looking at me quizzically, "am I wrong?"

Totally baffled, I returned her look. "Wrong about what?"

"Not to feel that I'm living a lie."

What bothered me about the question was that she was trying to vent her hostility on Al via me. I played mediator. "No, you're not wrong, but you don't want to live a lie either, right Al?"

Al replied haughtily, "Of course, I don't."

"Then why do you?" she asked pointedly.

He looked at her impatiently, spoke through clenched teeth. "Jill, will you please stop this damned nonsense about living a lie."

Jill's teeth were not clenched. She just yelled. "It is not nonsense to want to live honestly."

The look that Al gave me was candid bewilderment. As I looked from one to the other, I was suddenly flooded with a lot of thoughts. I realized that not only was there no love between Al and Jill, but that their very considerable mutual hostility was compounded by the fact that there was no communication either. Al's denial of his mother's alcoholism fueled Jill's anger because it was upon that denial that Al had constructed a prudish perception of Jill's role of wife and mother. The problem, I suddenly understood, was that, like many women, Jill saw herself cast into the role of her husband's mother. That is always bad. In this instance, it was much worse because Al wanted her to fulfill a role that his own mother had probably rejected. He wanted Jill to do for his kids everything his own mother had not done for him. Sadly, what those things were, he did not know. I was sure that this ignorance was a major reason for his bewilderment. As all these thoughts zipped through my head, I realized another. Jill, herself, coming as she did from an alcoholic home, in all likelihood had not had an especially effective role model for a mother. I nodded my head at Jill's last outburst. "I'm sure we all agree that it is not nonsense to want to live honestly. The problem, I think, has to do with agreeing on what is honest and what is not."

"Well," she said in a more modulated voice, "I don't think it's honest to lie to your kids about their grandparents, or about anything for that matter. Lies hurt kids."

My distinct impression was that Jill said it with enjoyment. Al must have had the same impression because this time it was he who yelled. "I don't and I never have lied to my kids!"

Jill bent toward him, her face masked in scorn. "That is pure crap," she said, "and if you don't know that, then you really are in trouble."

Al stood up. His usually beady eyes filled with anger looked positively saucerlike. "What lies? What lies? What lies have I ever told them?"

Jill, relaxed on the recliner, looked at him, unblinking, her expression calm and unemotional. "Everytime you give me that phoney little hug and kiss in front of them, you lie. Every gift you ever gave me was a lie. You don't love me. You never did. And you know it." Her voice had taken on a flat, dull quality. "And I take responsibility for some of it because I let you believe that I believed you did. The biggest tragedy of my miserable life is that I married you."

Al's reaction as she spoke was not feigned but real, pathetically so. Her words struck him so hard he fell back onto the couch. His reply came out in an astonished croak. "You don't love me!"

Maybe it was the genuineness of the astonishment. Maybe it was the utter commonplaceness of the words or the funny, squinched-up look on his face. Whatever the reason, the ardent poignancy of Jill's moment had dissolved with Al's croak. Suddenly the whole scene had taken on a crazy, satirical, comic quality. I felt as though I were in the middle of a badly overacted soap opera. Somehow I controlled my urge to laugh. Jill didn't. She exploded into a high-pitched howl.

"I don't see what's so funny," he said angrily.

That made Jill laugh harder. Worse, it made me laugh despite my efforts to control my mirth. What the scene had showed was that not only did Al lack a sense of humor but that probably he simply was out of touch much of the time, which is not uncommon for adult children of alcoholics. It also explained a little more why the two did not communicate very well. Apparently they were on different emotional wavelengths.

Jill stopped laughing. She looked at me. "God, that was funny!"

"I'm a riot," Al said, still angry.

"Well, I don't know about that but somehow I do feel relieved."

"I'm glad for you," he said with more than a hint of sarcasm.

Enough sarcasm, resentment, and naked hostility had been vented in the session. I knew now how each perceived and related to the other. Any more ventilation could only precipitate more negative feelings, perhaps even terminate the therapy for one or both of them. I stepped in. "What you were saying a moment ago, Jill, was pretty heavy stuff. Al was really floored by it." I nodded to him. "This is understandable, and Al," I said with all the kindness I could muster, "I wasn't, and I'm sure Jill wasn't, laughing at you or your feelings. More than anything, it was the moment. Sometimes we have to let out feelings, because we want relief from them. Laughing is a good way to do that, especially in a very tense moment." My thoughts were not original, certainly not profound, yet throughout my explanation Al's look had been one of puzzlement. Feelings, I concluded, were a mystery to Al. Again, this is not uncommon among children of alcoholics.

Jill's amused look turned to one of sadness. Then, in a voice that matched her look, she asked, "You don't know what he's talking about, do you Al?"

Al's response was an embarrassed shrug.

Both question and response spoke eloquently about their lack of relationship, about the frustration she must have endured over the years with a husband who was unable to express or accept feelings. I cleared my throat. "Let's go back to what you were saying a while ago, Jill."

She nodded, dully, I thought.

"You said that you were responsible for some of your difficulties because you let Al believe that you believed he loved you."

She sighed. "It's true. I did that."

"Why did you?" I asked.

She shook her head. "I'm not sure. Maybe because I was afraid to admit I had married a man who," she turned toward her husband, "no offense, Al, was not able to love."

The look on Al's face was alternately one of irritation and hurt. "You really think I don't love you, eh?"

Jill sighed again, spoke without any rancor. "I know you don't love me. But even if you did, you can't show it. So what does it matter?"

Al's look now was pure hurt. "I love you," he protested, "I do." The protest, however, was delivered in a small, weak voice.

Jill looked as though she wanted to cry. The ironic smile playing around her mouth imparted a clear and simple message. "See, I told you so!" I doubted if Al even saw the smile. "You were saying, Jill, that you fed into Al's inability to love because you were afraid to admit that you had married a man who couldn't love." I thought I knew the answer, but I wanted to hear her say it. "Why, Jill? Why were you afraid to admit that you had married a man who couldn't love?"

Al echoed the questions, "Yeah, why?"

"Dear God, what does it say about me?"

I pressed. "What?" I nodded toward Al. "Tell him."

"If nothing else," she said, turning toward her husband, "it means I don't think much of myself. It means, and I don't say it to hurt you, Al, but it means that I'm out of it just as much as you are."

Al's look told us both that he wasn't so much hurt by the comment as he was confused. This confusion, I was beginning to understand, was nothing more than a kind of denial. Unfortunately, it effectively insulated him against having to deal with feelings and information he didn't like. Her words had impressed me, reinforced what I had already learned. Jill might not have her husband's Dartmouth education but she was far more astute than he interpersonally and far more knowledgeable about his and her dynamics, and the dynamics of their relationship.

Then, inexplicably and without warning, and as so often happens in psychotherapy, a client's comments made my interpretative thoughts seem inaccurate and irrelevant.

Al expelled a loud sigh. His confused look dissipated as he talked in restrained, subdued tones. He kept his face averted from both Jill and me. "I know, I've always known that 'I'm out of it,' as you put it, and I know that I don't have a sense of humor. I go to parties and I see people having a good time, and if you want to know, it drives me crazy. In my entire life, I have never had a good time at a party. The simple truth is that I don't know how. But that doesn't mean I don't want to. I do. I want to. But Jill," he said, looking at her fully, "none of that means I don't love you. I give you those presents you call phoney because it's my way. You may not believe it, but I spend a lot of time thinking and planning what to get you. I don't mind that because love is inconvenient. Anyway, I never realized that you thought they were phoney. And when I kiss you in front of the kids, you're right, I do it on purpose. I think it's nice for kids to see their father kiss their mother, probably," he said suddenly, averting his face again, "because I never saw too much of that in my own house."

The look on Jill's face was beyond surprise. It could well have been shock. Her mouth worked to say something. Nothing came out. I chuckled. I do that when tension builds. Neither of them responded to the chuckle, probably because neither noticed it.

"That," she said in a funny choked voice, "is the first time you ever really talked to me."

"Probably true," he said with embarrassment. "But, Jill, honest to' God, all I want to do is talk to you and be honest with you. You make it hard, too. You don't talk to me. You're, how to put it, distant. You've grown very distant in the past year, maybe longer, I don't know."

Jill had begun to look guilty. She nodded. "It's true that I have but it's probably because I got used to being alone, thinking alone, even talking alone."

"You have the kids," he said.

"I love my kids. But a woman needs more than her kids, especially when she's supposed to have a husband."

I sensed a lot of hidden meaning in Jill's last words, debated for a second whether it was prudent to probe, then decided to. "You're saying that you were lonely for adult companionship."

"Yes," she said. "For someone to talk to, share things with. I've always been needy in that area. Al seems to get along very well being alone.

"But I don't," he protested. "I'm lonely, too. I'm probably a lonelier person than you are!"

"Well, why are you never home?"

"Because we need the money."

"I'll work. I'll be happy to work."

Al's next words were predictable. "And you know very well I don't want you to."

We had come full circle. "Look," I said, "we're on a silly kind of merry-go-round now. We're just not getting anywhere. A few moments ago, you were both saying you were lonely people. Help me understand how come you're both lonely when you both claim you don't want to be?"

They looked at each other, then at me. Jill spoke. "I don't know," she said looking at Al, "and to be honest about it, it isn't just that. Al's out a lot because even when he's home I feel lonely. Don't you?" she asked.

He nodded. "Yeah, guess so."

"No communication," she said lightly, "Maybe it's that we're very private people."

I looked from one to the other. "Tell me, were you both always 'very private people'?"

There was a long pause. Al was looking at me intently, and seemed to be mulling over the question. He nodded. "Yeah, it's true. I've always been a very private person."

I responded quickly, without thinking. "So private you never let your wife into your life." Having said that, I wondered if I might have overstepped.

Apparently not, because Al nodded as he looked at Jill. "It's true, I've shut you out, haven't I?"

Jill snapped her response. "Stop feeling guilty. We're both to blame, not just you."

The tone surprised me. Up to this point, I'd felt very much on Jill's wavelength. All the emotions she had emitted had been eminently appropriate, or at least very understandable. Incongruous behavior intrigues me. I pursued it. "Why do you think you just spoke irritatedly?"

"I don't know." She looked at Al. "I'm sorry."

I thought she might know, had just avoided the question. For some reason, I felt she just didn't want to pursue the topic. I debated a few seconds, then went with the question I wanted to ask. "How private are you, Jill."

She looked right into my eyes and answered cooly, "Very private." Both voice and look told me she was not going to explain that today.

It didn't matter. Our time was up.

Reflections

One of the most unusual aspects of this couple is that both displayed sharp inconsistencies in their personalities. When we began the session, all the dynamics indicated that Al was the denier par excellence while Jill was the one beset with a vital concern for what was true and for not living a lie. When the session ended, I had the distinct impression that Al was struggling mightily to overcome his denial while Jill was covering up or holding back an important truth.

There is much that distresses me about this case. Basically, the problems are founded in how Jill's role should be viewed. Al's acute need is to have Jill function as an ideal wife and mother. Such a view angers and depresses Jill, and makes her feel trapped and useless. Al's need stems not only from the fact of his alcoholic mother, but also from his problems with his lack of self-esteem as a man. His insistence that Jill not go to work but stay at home and play homemaker full time could also be a function of his "insane jealousy" which he did not deny nor did he even respond to the allegation. But it was his lack of response when Jill referred to him as "a sick bull" (a term especially rich in sexual implication) that really pointed up the low regard in which he holds himself as a man. These thoughts, combined with the incredible hostility each showed to the other, make me believe that their sex life cannot be very good. It is something we will have to address.

The major concern is the lack of communication, verbally and emotionally. In this regard, they are stereotypical of adult children of alcoholics. Despite Al's dramatic emotional self-disclosure (he even touched on the lack of love displayed at home by his parents), it is very clear that he is not used to showing or accepting emotion. What makes this lack of communication especially serious, however, is that it has gone

on for a very long time. Put simply, Al and Jill are used to not com-
municating. This fact gives fuller meaning to Jill's explanation about
being "very private people." What she was saying was that people
necessarily become private when they live with aloneness. What I wonder
is whether they have adjusted to their aloneness. If they have, the prog-
nosis for the rehabilitation of this marriage is poor.

The next session was with Jill alone. Al had called in the afternoon to tell me he couldn't make it, "I've got a good-sized deal cooking. I've got a half a city block I'm brokering. We'll both make the
next session, I promise. By the way, doctor, I want you to know that
I really did enjoy the other night. Enjoyed it a lot. Really got a lot
out of it. You're a good counselor. Thanks."

Effusiveness irks me. It usually makes me wonder what it's covering up. Right now, it made me wonder if the cancellation was
necessary. My wonder was fueled by Jill's comment when I opened
the door to her that evening. "Did you hear about my friend?" she
asked.

I nodded, and using some of his words, told her what he had said.

Jill made a face. "He's always got a 'good-sized deal cooking.' It's
his way of letting you know that he's an important person."

She was wearing her hair differently, parted in the middle and
pulled back tightly into a bun. The style, while a little passe, highlighted
her high cheek bones and imparted a sophisticated effect despite the
gray slacks and blue and white sweater.

"When we finished last time," I said, "you were telling me that
you are a very private person."

"True. I am."

"Been like that all your life?"

She nodded. "All my life. Probably because I was brought up in
a three-bedroom house with six brothers and sisters and one bathroom.
There was no privacy. Even so, I kept my privacy. It wasn't that hard.
In a family with an alcoholic father, there's a lot of aloneness even
when you sleep in a bed with two sisters."

"You weren't close to your family?"

"No, and not now either. We never see them."

"What do you remember about your father's house?"

"Mostly being afraid. I was afraid a lot."

"What were you afraid of?"

She shook her head. "Everything and nothing."

I gave her a questioning look.

She smiled. "I was afraid of people—kids, teachers, my brothers,
and especially my two older sisters."

Curious, I thought, she hadn't mentioned either mother or father. "What about your parents?"

"Yeah, I was scared of my mother, but I was positively terrified of my father."

"Why? Did he abuse you?"

"No."

"Did he abuse your brothers and sisters?"

She shook her head, gave me a funny little smile. "I guess I was born scared, eh?"

"Nobody," I said with pure conviction, "is born scared. Fear is learned. Tell me, how did your father act at home? Did he yell a lot or was he mostly quiet?"

"He yelled really loud, but mostly he was quiet."

I shook my head. "Run that by me again."

"When he yelled, he really roared. I was petrified when he did that. He didn't do it much though."

"What does that mean?"

"I'm not sure, but I guess that was what bothered me, what scared me, was that none of us knew when it was going to happen."

Now I understood. What she had been calling fear was really anxiety. Unpredictability precipitates anxiety. Explosive tempers are totally unpredictable, especially when it is liquor that is fueling the explosions. I related my thoughts. "So you see, what you've been telling me is that basically you were a very anxious little kid. You mentioned teachers before. I'll bet being in school made you especially anxious."

She nodded. "You're right. It did. How did you know that?"

"Teachers evaluate. Anxious kids can't bear to be evaluated."

She nodded. "True. I remember my last day of school in the fourth grade. I got to school early, very early, maybe 7:30, and walking around the school yard alone, my heart beating like a hammer, I started crying. I was terrified."

"Why?"

"I was afraid I wasn't going to pass." She looked away. Her eyes had teared up while she relived those painful moments. "I still wonder why I was so anxious because the truth is that nobody would even have cared if I had been kept back. I don't remember my mother or father even once asking me how I did or what I did in school."

"Who signed your report card?"

"After sixth grade, I signed it. Before that, one of my sisters would sign it. We thought it was all a joke. Looking back now, it wasn't a joke. It wasn't funny. It was tragic." She wiped her eyes. "I'm only now beginning to realize how anxious I really was. I think the worst was when I was in the seventh grade. That was the year we had a hearing test. We put on earphones and we were supposed to write down the letters and numbers we heard. I flunked that test three times. The school doctor sent me to a hearing doctor, who found nothing wrong with my ears."

"It was all anxiety," I said.

She nodded. "Whenever I had to take a test, I died a little bit because I knew I was going to fail."

What she was really telling me was that, like most children reared in an alcoholic home, she had severe problems with her self-esteem. "What I'm learning from what you're telling me is that you were really beaten down at home."

"I guess so, but not so as you'd notice."

My look told her I thought it was a curious response. "Like I told you, nobody beat me up physically, and nobody beat me up by putting me down either. You know why I was a wreck as a kid?"

"Why?"

"Because nobody paid any attention to me."

I nodded in agreement. "The worse put-down of all is indifference."

"Yeah. You're not going to believe this I know, but I never really knew I was pretty. I'm only now beginning to understand it."

"I believe you." I did because it all fit. Now I understood why she had married Al.

She paused, searched my eyes. "You know, Al was the very first person to tell me I was pretty. I was so grateful for that, and so starved for affection that I married him. And I married him because I couldn't believe I'd ever find anybody else who would marry me. And I did so want to get out of that crazy house. And look, look what I've done. I've created my own crazy house. I think about that all the time."

Her voice had become lower and lower until now she was at a whisper. The voice, together with her expression, gave me the distinct impression that the words she had just uttered were all too familiar, that she was not so much talking to me as replaying very familiar thoughts out loud. I told her my impression.

She smiled. "You're right. Anyway, I am what I am and I've done what I've done because all my life I've been living in an indifferent world."

"You said before that Al told you you were pretty."

She smiled. "I told my mother that and you know what she said? She said, 'My God, Jill, that boy's so homely everybody's got to look pretty to him.' Nice thing for a mother to say, eh?"

"She never told you you were pretty?"

Jill shook her head. "My mother never had time for me, my mother never told me anything. A couple of years ago, I told her that—that she had never once complimented me in my whole life. You know what she said? She said, well, I never told you you were ugly, did I? Nice, huh? I should be grateful that she never told me I was ugly. God!" She wiped her eyes with a tissue.

I verbalized what I thought she might be feeling, "A lot worse than not being told you're ugly is never to be told you're beautiful."

Jill burst into tears. "It's all right. It's all right," she sobbed. "I'll be all right in a minute. Just give me a minute."

I shrugged. "Take five if you want."

"I couldn't cry for five minutes if I wanted to," she blubbered dabbing at her eyes.

"Why not?" I asked.

"Feeling sorry for myself is one problem I don't have. Probably the only one." Her tears stopped. "I feel better," she said with a little embarrassed laugh.

"Good! A little while ago you said that you're only now beginning to understand or appreciate that you're pretty."

"Yeah?" A wary look had suddenly come into Jill's eyes, as if she knew what my next question was going to be.

I asked it. "Any special reason after all these years why you should begin to feel that you're pretty?"

She shrugged. "Maybe I'm just a late bloomer. I don't know. You're the doctor, you tell me."

I had my suspicions but I couldn't express them quite yet. I leaned back. It didn't make sense that she would begin to appreciate her physical attractiveness in her present circumstances. It is people who make people feel beautiful. It certainly was not Al doing that. Someone else had to be. Yes, Jill was having an affair. I debated for a moment about confronting her, but decided that, despite our very good rapport, she probably felt that our relationship was not yet such that she could make such a major disclosure. In any case, I couldn't risk it. If she denied it, the therapy, for all intents and purposes, would be over. "Even though you know I have impressions, I'd like you to tell me what you think and feel about Al."

"What you are asking me is what I think about our marriage?"

I sensed that she had a good feeling about what I was edging toward. Even so, I continued playing the little game. Most children of alcoholics, being used to denial, seem to handle it pretty well. I nodded. "I guess that's what I'm asking you."

She looked away, sighed dispiritedly. "It's like most marriages, it could be better."

"It could be better?"

"We probably fight too much. There's probably too much anger between us. You saw us. What do you think?"

I nodded in agreement. "A lot of anger."

"Yes."

"Why do you think there's so much?" If she could admit to the why, she'd probably admit to the affair.

"That's easy. Ask me something hard."

Without intending to, I gave her a quasiquizzical look. Was her request a veiled invitation? Even so, I wanted to be on the safest of ground. I continued with my little game. "Tell me, why so much anger?"

"Not too much love."

"Why not?"

"He doesn't know how and I just can't seem to love him, and God knows I have tried! For 15 years now, I have tried."

As earlier, when she had literally whispered her response to me, I had the distinct impression that this was a realization Jill had replayed in her mind many, many times.

I reaffirmed her conviction, "For 15 years you have tried."

"I just can't seem to."

"But you married him?"

"I told you," she said with a totally candid look, "that he was the first, the only, man or person who gave me attention. He was a college graduate. His family had money. God! All the wrong reasons, huh?"

"People marry for those reasons."

"It took me almost five years to realize I didn't love him. Then I spent five years depressed because I realized the only thing that kept me sane was keeping busy as a mother."

Her way of explaining the years with Al still seemed to contain the unconscious veiled invitation to ask my question. I explored. "So, how's it been for you for the past five years?"

She looked away. "I guess I've adjusted to the whole mess."

"You've adjusted?"

"Yes."

I leaned back. She reminded me of a child on the beach, fascinated and conflicted by the lapping tide, desperately wanting to know what it would be like to get wet by the waves but too scared to find out. "For five years now you've been adjusted to an unhappy marriage?'

She nodded.

"During these five years, you've grown used to the idea of spending the rest of your life with a man whom you can't love?"

She nodded again, said "yes" with more than a bit of anger.

I decided then to ask the question which, although not very confrontative, would probably get us to where we needed to go. "Tell me," I asked crisply, "what's it like sexually for you with Al?"

The sudden relief on her face told me that she preferred this to a head-on confrontation. "I was wondering when you would ask me that."

I shrugged. "I'm asking."

She looked me straight in the eyes and told me. "We haven't had sex for, I don't know, five or six years."

For some reason that surprised me. "No sex at all?"

"No."

"Where does he sleep?"

"Where? Why with me. We've only got three bedrooms."

I could appreciate why she was not volunteering more. It was more than a little embarrassing for her and making me ask questions was providing her with more time to deal with the larger issue. "Twin beds or double bed?"

"Double bed. And I know what you're thinking. You sleep in the same bed and never have sex?"

"I was thinking that, yes."

She paused a moment. "Have you ever heard of that before, married people sleeping together and never doing it?"

I nodded. "Yes," then added lightly, "only married people could, not lovers."

She grinned. "For sure!"

The verve of her reply told me that she was edging closer to the core topic. I could wait.

"Obviously you had sex in the beginning, when you were first married."

"Obviously," she said with a hint of condescension. "Bill and Penny are alive."

I ignored the condescension and asked pleasantly. "What happened?"

"I really don't know," she said, her puzzlement genuine. "We just grew more and more distant from each other."

"How was it with him, Jill?"

She gave me an ironic look. "What would you guess, doctor?"

"Not very good."

"Correct! And you want to hear something? I didn't really know it wasn't. I suspected he wasn't a very good lover as every woman must with a jerk, but I didn't really know. I was a virgin when I got married. Anyway, I just accepted the mechanical, routine way it was with him. For a long time I thought that it was supposed to be like that."

She had edged close enough. I asked the question. "Then you found out?"

Despite the veiled invitations and allusions, her head actually snapped back at the query. She looked down, "Yeah," she said in a small, soft voice. "I found out."

"You want to tell me?"

Several moments passed. She looked up. The conflict was reflected on her face, in the sadness in her eyes, and in the little smile that played around her mouth. The smile broadened. "I've never talked to anybody about it." There was a long pause. It reflected not so much embarrassment as the strangeness she felt. "There are so few with whom one can talk about an affair."

I waited.

She looked up at me. The smile had faded but the sadness in her eyes remained. "I can't give him up."

My shrug told her that I did not see it as my business to try to talk her into doing that.

"He's a tremendous person." Those were her words. Her tone did not fit them. It was detached, objective, unemotional. She related how they had met at a neighborhood party. "He lives just down the street."

"He's married then?"

"Yes, and that's what bothers me most about the whole thing, that he's married."

"Why does that bother you?"

"His wife might find out. I'm not interested in hurting her and in maybe breaking up a family."

"Are you able to see each other much?"

She nodded. "I'm home alone. His wife works. Gets a little sticky to see him during school vacations because all the kids are home, but we manage."

Lovers, I thought with an inward smile, always manage. "You must feel pressured trying to see him at times, especially in the summer."

She nodded. "I do. But it's all worth it. He makes my life bearable, and when I'm with him it's positively exciting."

"You're more than willing to put up with any anxieties it might cause you?"

"Any," she said, "and I have put up with a lot, juggling schedules and vacation days. It would all be much easier if I could work. I'd have more freedom. I wouldn't be expected to be home all the time and I would not have to be so damned accountable for my time."

"Have you thought of a divorce?"

"We have. He and I talk about it every once in a while. We just can't. We're afraid of the effects on the kids. We've decided to wait."

As she talked, I couldn't help thinking about her comments during the previous session when she had chastised her husband about living a lie, when she had spoken almost arrogantly about the need to live life honestly. Attributing to another the behaviors and attitudes one harbors oneself is fairly typical of the adult child of alcoholics. Attributing like this is not hypocrisy because it is not premeditated. It is done more unconsciously than consciously. It is a defense, and it even has a name—projection. "Would you like to marry this man?"

"I'd love to, but like I said, we've decided to wait."

"How long has it been going on?"

"About three months."

That startled me. The way she spoke had implied that it had been a long-term affair. I had a sudden thought. "Jill, have there been other men?"

She nodded, her expression matter of fact. "Yes."

"How many?"

"Two."

Much was getting clearer for me, but much was more confused. I leaned forward, "When did the first one occur?"

"I'm not sure, maybe four or five years ago."

I observed, flatly, "This is your third affair in four or five years?"

"Yes."

I paused, spoke slowly, "Help me understand. . . ."

She interrupted, a wry grin on her face, "What you want to know is, why? Why do I let lovers come and go but stay with a husband I don't like?"

She had thought about this. "Yes."

"I don't know why exactly. All I know is that I can't stand Al but I don't want to divorce him."

"You said something about the effect on the children before."

"That's not the only reason."

"What's the reason?"

The vulnerable look jibed perfectly with her words. "I'm scared to divorce him. I haven't worked in 15 years and then I was only a file clerk. What would I do? How would I live? I've never even paid a bill in my whole life. I left my father's house, not much of a house, but a house and went into Al's. I have never been on my own. I'm scared," she repeated. She said all that very fast, paused a moment, then added. "Besides, the first two guys had just come out of divorces themselves. The last thing they wanted was to get married. And like I told you, this one is married."

"Why the breakups with the first two?"

She shook her head. "I really don't know. They just sort of ended. I lost interest. They did too, I think." She shrugged, "My lovers don't last. Only my husband does."

I leaned back and thought about all she had told me. "Jill, is your life such now that you need to have an affair?"

I thought my question would surprise her. It didn't. "I don't want it to be like that," she said.

"I'm sure you don't. But my question was. . . ."

She interrupted testily. "I heard your question. I had that very thought after my second affair started. After this one started, I decided that it's true. I need to have an affair to escape the boredom of my life. It's awful I know, but I think I have affairs just because I don't know what else to do. It's like I have to have an affair to stay sane!"

"Do you care for these men while you're seeing them?"

"Yes."

"Do you feel bad when you break up with them?"

"After the first one I did, yes. I cried."

"Not so bad after the second, though?"

"No, not so bad. Like a lot of things it only hurts bad the first time." She said that almost brightly.

I understood that. "Did you break up with them or did they break up with you? How did it go?"

"Mutual."

"Why did you break up?"

"No special reason. We lost interest in each other."

I believed her. Therapy has taught me this is the prime reason affairs end.

She paused, "You know, I never drank alone. I never even drank to get myself feeling good until after my first affair ended. I got drunk at a party the night after we broke up. I did the same kind of thing after my second breakup. I don't do that when I'm having an affair. I don't want to drink when I'm having an affair. In fact, I don't seem to want anything when I'm having an affair." She looked at me, eyes shining. "Affairs are exciting."

I wanted to be sure she meant that, so I repeated her words. "Affairs are exciting."

"Yes!"

"You sound a little like you get high on them."

"It's true, I do." She smiled.

"But then when it's over you have to come down."

"Yeah." The smile faded. "I have to come down. That's when it would really be nice to talk to someone. Even so, I'm grateful to be able to talk like this now. I mean, who can you talk to about an affair when you're a married woman?"

"I suspect some women talk to close friends."

"I don't have any, never really did."

She paused, then verbalized the thought that, ironically, I'd had on my mind for the past several minutes. "I think Al suspects."

I have seldom encountered an affair that wasn't at least suspected at some level by the other spouse. Whether or not Al was aware was difficult to fathom. On the one hand, he was an incredible denier but at the same time he was inordinately suspicious and jealous. Al's suspiciousness seemed an integral part of his personality. What I wondered now was what part she had played in precipitating the jealousy. "Why do you think he suspects?"

"Little things."

"Specifically?"

"He calls me at odd hours. I know he's checking up on me."

"How do you know that?"

"For one thing, he really doesn't have anything to say. He just says, 'Hi,' and later explains it's his way of telling me he loves me." She paused a moment, looked very thoughtful. "Mostly it's the way he treats me."

"How's that?"

"Well, even though he's more suspicious and acts more jealous than ever—I mean, my God, at a party he drives me and everybody else crazy the way he looks at me and the way he hovers over me— even so, afterward he's incredibly solicitous. I mean, he opens car doors for me, brings me little presents. He never used to be like that. He was always suspicious, always a little jealous, but never solicitous. He wasn't like that even before we were married."

"So what does all that mean to you?"

"It means he knows."

"But doesn't want to admit it?"

She shook her head. "I think he knows. I think he knows and it scares him."

She was confirming what I had believed for a while.

"I boost his ego. He loves showing me off. And even though we don't have any friends, we're always going to and giving parties. He says it's for his business, to make contacts. I know better. He likes to show me off."

"What you're saying is that basically he doesn't want a divorce?"

"A divorce," she drawled with positive satisfaction, "would kill him."

"You told me before that it scared you, too."

She sighed, nodded slowly, "Two scared people. What you have on your hands are two scared people."

Unhappily married people who are too scared to divorce are not that rare. What made this situation different was that while both were too scared to divorce, neither was interested enough in the relationship to take charge of it. This is unique because, in most marital relationships, regardless of the relationship's quality, one is in charge, or at least has the greater control. In this one, neither was in charge and neither was willing or able to assume control. Their fears prevented it—her fear that she would have to cope with life alone and his that he would lose status. And so Jill and Al found themselves feeding each other's neurosis with their fears, found themselves playing roles they both detested—she that of a wife and he that of an unknowing, cuckolded husband.

Apparently attuned to my thoughts, she interrupted them. "It's all very depressing, isn't it?"

I answered slowly, seriously. "Not for me to say. The whole situation can be depressing if you don't want to find a solution. My impression right now is that you feel trapped, as you said in the session with Al."

"I am. I'm trapped," she cried.

"Only if you choose to be," I said with conviction.

"What are my choices?"

We spent the rest of this session and the next four discussing them. Finally we saw only two: to face her fears and file for divorce or to continue to have affairs to mitigate her unhappiness in her marriage. My impression after these sessions was that she was going to go with what she perceived to be the easier path. The affair with its excitement, together with the flattering attention she got from another man, seemed easier and preferable to trying to cope with life alone.

I pointed out that there might be subtle, insidious effects on her general self-regard were she to continue a life of affairs.

"I don't agree," she said crisply, "that I'm going to think less and less about myself after a while because I'm having an affair. Affair or no affair, I never felt too good about myself anyway. Truth is I feel best about myself when I'm having an affair. To be honest, I don't see anything that wrong about it. I'm always very discreet. And crazy as it may seem, I feel better toward Al when I'm having an affair. Anyway, I seem to want to treat him better. I mean, who am I hurting really?"

I was tempted to respond not so much with statements, but with questions dealing with what she had talked about so eloquently at our first session—about the need not to live a lie. However, the fear of having to be totally responsible for herself and to parent her children alone was overwhelming. At this time at least, she was not ready to change the course of her life. I didn't prolong the discussion as we would just be going over the same material.

Al meanwhile continued making appointments, then canceling them, a certain indication that he wasn't interested in making any changes either. What bothered me most about it all was that I was beginning to feel as though I was wasting my time—even worse, that I was becoming part of their neurotic dynamics. Thus, she, by seeing me, and he, by just making appointments, were doing nothing more than feeding their denial systems. Mere contact with me was telling them that everything was really O.K. They could feel that they were doing the best they could to deal with their problems, or at the very least, they were working on them. In short, I was becoming a psychotherapeutic patsy! It was for this reason that, when Al called, I told him that if he chose to cancel again, I would not make any more appointments with him, or with his wife either.

"Oh wow," he exclaimed, "you won't help us anymore?"

"Al," I said with studied calm, "I've seen Jill five times. I've gone as far as I can with her alone. I now need to see you alone just to get to know a comparable amount about you. If I can do that, I would then like to see you two together again with the kids. After that we'll go from there. But again, first I need to see you alone."

He answered by telling me he would get back to me.

Reflections

Reared in an alcoholic family, Jill learned to live as a scared, insecure, and anxious girl. Familial interaction provided few rewards, little recognition, and even less enhancement. The prime mode of communication in her home was cruel indifference. Her way of life today as a woman can be understood as a response to that rearing.

Her emotional deprivation was so acute while she was growing up that she married Al because he was the first person to give her any attention. Her affairs began when that attention ceased, when the atmosphere of indifference with Al became comparable to the atmosphere in which she had been reared. The affairs continue not only because they flatter, but because they provide the antidote to the depression and anxiety she experienced as a child.

The positive feelings she expressed about the affair were honest, and the dynamics of this kind of relationship fit well with those of an adult child of an alcoholic home. Indeed, Jill sees such a relationship as ideal because there doesn't have to be any involvement. She can stay in an affair as long as she wants, and get out of it when she wants. Implied strongly in her view is that commitment to a lover is a function of interest, need, and mood. Note: she picked lovers of a disposition comparable to her's—none of them were interested in marriage.

Finally, Jill can maintain her view of the affair and continue her way of life because Al's needs feed hers. To Jill, he is an ideal husband. Thus, while she may find him boring, infuriating, and at times even revolting, he is also a security blanket who insulates her from a reality with which she is inexperienced and which she perceives as harsh and cruel.

I am not optimistic about the prognosis for healthful changes in either of them. There seems to be more reward in their continuing in their neurotic but secure ways than in entering a transition period leading to basic changes.

My best judgment is that Al will not call me.

My best judgment proved wrong. Al called, made an appointment, and showed up for it.

"Doctor, I want you to know I am sorry for all the confusion but business has been crazy, just crazy for the past month."

Tone and expression flat, noncommittal, I let the irony of my words tell him I wasn't buying his excuse. "It was all out of your hands that you had to cancel four times in a row?"

He flushed. "Yeah, right." Then throwing himself into the two-seater couch, he added with a pout, "Anyway I'm here."

I confronted the pout. "You don't sound as though you're too happy about it."

"Quite the contrary, I'm glad to be here," he said, with his best salesman smile. "All I want to do is help."

"Al," I said patiently, "I'm the one who is supposed to help."

"I meant my wife. I want to help her," he said solemnly.

"She's the one with the problem?"

He nodded. "She's the alcoholic."

I didn't answer for a couple of moments. The expression on his face was honest and serious. If nothing else, my sessions with Jill had convinced me that she had told me the truth, that she resorted to alcohol only between affairs. Her alcoholic-like drinking, if it was that, was very much a function of the relationship, or, more accurately, the lack of a relationship with her husband. The problem was going to be to get him to see that, and apparently Al, staunch and classic denier that he was, did not want to see that at all. Nevertheless, I had to give it a try. "You don't see where you might be a factor in her drinking?"

"Nobody," he said with certainty, "ever made anybody alcoholic."

Amazing, I thought, how much comfort, solace, and justification one can find in an abstract idea. I nodded. "You're probably right, Al, nobody ever made anybody alcoholic." Then I just said it. "I'm not so sure that Jill is alcoholic even though she may have been drunk a few times in the past four or five years, but that's not the question I asked you."

"What did you ask me?" The candid look on his face indicated clearly that he didn't know what I had asked. It fit. Al heard only what he wanted to hear.

"Do you feel your relationship might be causing her to drink to excess once in a while?"

"What's our relationship got to do with the fact that she gets drunk?"

I knew I could duel with him, point out that she had drunk to excess only a few times at parties, but he wouldn't admit to it because he didn't see it, precisely because he couldn't permit himself to. Moreover, I couldn't tell him that she drank while in the hangover of an affair. I addressed the problem in a roundabout manner. "How do you see your relationship?"

He looked at me suspiciously. "Doctor, I know you've been seeing her. I'm not sure what she's been saying but I can guess."

"Al," I said impatiently, "you've told me that all you want to do is help but you have yet to answer a question. I'll repeat it, how do you see your relationship with Jill?"

His first words surprised me. "Not so good. You have to know that. You've heard how she feels about me, I'm sure." His next words didn't surprise me at all. "It's the booze that makes her feel and act like that toward me, right?"

I know how powerful denial can be. Even so, I shook my head. He apparently didn't notice because he went on.

"The reason I say that is that she's been treating me and the kids much, much better. I notice, and I've gone out of my way to notice, that she's hardly drinking at all lately. I'm convinced it's all related."

I nodded. "Yes, Al, it's all related."

"And I think this therapy with you has really helped, really helped. I want to thank you for that. What do you think? It's the drink that makes her feel and act lousy toward me, right?"

I settled back in my chair, debated for a second whether to hit him with the truth—and hit him it would. Even though my style is basically candid and confrontative, I have no stomach for unkindness.

This I realized was one of those times when candor bordered on cruelty. At the same time, I couldn't let him wallow blithely in his world of fantasy and denial. I sighed and went to candor. "You have it backward."

His brows shot up. "Backward?"

"Backward," I said softly.

"You mean she drinks because she doesn't love me? Is that what you're saying?"

"That's what I'm saying."

"Well," he said brightly, "I noticed that she's got the drink pretty much under control lately. She's been treating me much better, too. How do you explain that, the therapy?"

"It could be that, yes." I couldn't tell him about the affair. To do so would have been to violate Jill's confidentiality. I find myself playing this kind of a game periodically in couple therapy when one of them has divulged a confidence to which the other is not privy. In such cases, the confidence is disclosed before termination. I doubted that it would be in this case, given the importance to Jill to be in an ever-continuing affair. At this point, all I could do was talk around it and focus on the reason I had asked to see him alone. "What we haven't talked about Al, is what it was like for you growing up. What your parents were like. You haven't told me about them."

"They were good parents, both of them," he said in a stilted and defensive tone.

I continued, "Last time the three of us met, Jill said your mother was alcoholic."

He nodded. "Yeah, she had a drinking problem. She drank more than she should now and then."

"She spent a lot of time in some kind of treatment center?"

He nodded. "She had to go away four times, maybe five. I'm not sure."

I leaned forward, "Al, how can a mother who's under the weather periodically be a, quote, good mother? As best and as honestly as you can remember now, how was she as a mother?"

"I've always been honest with you," he said in a voice that also said, "How can you think for a second I've ever lied to you?"

"I know you have been. Call it a figure of speech. Anyway, how was she as a mother?"

He looked away. "I remember a psychology professor in college saying that how far back we can remember in our lives is an indication of how much loving treatment we got as little babies. Most people, he said, have little sunny tableaus they carry around in their heads that go back to when they were two and a half or three."

"So?"

"So, I don't have a single tableau in my head. In fact, I've never been able to remember anything before first grade. Best I can figure it, my memories start around six or seven, and they are not sunny. They're dark."

"What you're telling me, Al, is that you didn't get a lot of loving treatment as a little kid."

"No," he said, with a funny little catch in his voice, "I guess I didn't."

"Do you know why?"

"My parents fought a lot. Maybe it was due to my mother's drinking. I don't know. My father used to yell a lot about it and she would scream back awful stuff."

"What kind of awful stuff?"

"Put-down stuff mostly, because he was never home."

I sensed that there was much more, and that he wanted desperately to share it but couldn't just yet.

"Your father was out a lot?"

He nodded. "He worked very hard. He was a successful man. We were about the richest folks in town."

"Not the happiest though, eh?"

He sighed. "No, not the happiest."

He spent the next quarter of an hour describing a home where there was little love or caring, where the parents lived apart from each other and from him. "It was true that my father was never home. I went days without seeing him, but even though my mother was home, she really wasn't because I never saw her either. She stayed in her room all the time. I've never been sure why, all I know is that I don't remember my mother in the kitchen or in the livingroom. I remember her in the bedroom, in bed, sick, and I never could bother her. The shades were usually down and it was dark except for a night light right next to the door as you came in. Sometimes the TV was on. Once when she came home from the hospital at Christmas, she sat in the living room with me. I was so used to seeing her only in her bedroom that I remember thinking she just didn't look right sitting on the small couch in front of the fireplace. I remember thinking that she just didn't belong there, that she belonged in bed, in her room."

"What you have been telling me is that she never functioned as a mother, but somebody must have taken care of you when you were a child."

"Baby sitters. Lots and lots of sitters. For some reason, they never lasted. For the longest time I thought there was something the matter with me. I realize now either my father or mother, and usually my father, found something wrong with them. My mother just didn't care. My father was a fussy and particular man. He was like that for the cleaning woman and especially for the cook. We had just about every woman in town who worked as a domestic work for us at one time or another. It got so he had to bring them in from the next town."

There was a long pause as Al reflected on what he had said.

"The way you talked before, I had the impression that your mother had her own room."

He nodded.

"So your parents didn't sleep together?"

"No, I guess they didn't. You know," he said with a funny smile, "I never knew until much later that most married people did. I think I learned that from watching movies."

Again I sensed something, an important something, unsaid. Softly I asked, "Al, what was there between your mother and father?"

"What do you mean?"

"Well, you describe your mother as a recluse, uninterested in you, her home, or her husband. Was it because she was alcoholic?" If I stopped right there, I might have gotten the answer. I didn't though and instead stupidly I asked another question. "Did you see her drunk a lot?"

"No. I just didn't see her like that but she was in the house all the time. I heard her moving around."

"So she stayed in her darkened room with the shades drawn. How do you know she was drunk? How did she get her liquor? Who brought her her meals?"

"Cleaning women brought her her meals. I did sometimes."

"What about the booze?"

He shrugged. "I don't know about that. Every once in a while my father ranted at her that she was drunk. Those were bad fights. They seemed to happen most when I was in junior high school. Then after I started Exeter, I just never saw her much, or him either, except at Christmas, which was awful because we all tried to act like everything was fine."

"Was your mother boozed up for the holidays?"

"My mother was never staggering drunk, but I know now that she had the smell of an alcoholic."

"What did she smell like?"

"Eucalyptus cough drops mixed with gin. As a kid I just accepted that. Only in the last years have I realized that it's the smell of an alcoholic. Anyway, at Christmas it was awful because it was apparent to me that my parents didn't even like each other because after I arrived and we had our first hellos, they just ignored each other, and me as well."

I asked the obvious question, "Why didn't they divorce?"

"I really don't know. Maybe because we were Catholic. I don't know."

When I asked him to tell me more about his father, he repeated that he was absent much of the time and that he was very fussy but also was very hard working and successful. "My father was a very serious man with little sense of humor. In fact, I never saw him laugh. I was never able to please him even though I worked hard in school and got decent grades. I wanted to go into business with him. A lot of kids don't want to go into the family business. I did. He didn't want me to, said I should make my own success. So I went into teaching. He didn't approve of that either, forever repeating the Shaw line about 'those who can do and those who can't teach.' It's funny but it wasn't until after he died that I began doing what he had done, selling real estate. Funny, eh?"

I didn't respond to that but asked the question I had been wanting to ask. For some reason I did it warily and in a low voice. "Did you like your father, Al?"

The look he gave me was a blend of surprise and conflict. He shrugged. "I never thought about it."

"Think about it."

Al moved back in his chair like he wanted to move away from the question. Several moments passed. Finally he said, "I never really knew him."

I nodded. "Probably true. What you were saying about him a few moments ago gave me that impression. At the same time, Al, the man you described strikes me as being much like you."

Al's eyes had widened. "What?"

"Very serious, didn't laugh much, never home, hard working, and a few other things. Correct me if I'm wrong. Isn't that very much you?"

"Are you saying that I'm like my father?"

It was transparent that he didn't want to be like his father, and too, that I had offended him. He was hurt and angry. "Al," I said pleasantly, "the characteristics you spoke of a few minutes. . . ."

His interruption was literally shouted. "I am not my father!"

"I didn't say. . . ."

"I am not a fag!"

That left me with my mouth open.

He fell back on the couch. I waited for him to speak.

His voice came out choked. "I always knew it but never said it. Would you believe it, never thought it even?"

I cleared my throat, "Yes, I believe it."

"Once when I was in elementary school, in the fifth grade, I was in my room reading *Paul Bunyan*. I even know the chapter. Paul Bunyan on Onion River. Anyway, my father started screaming at my mother that she was a lousy lush. Then there was an awful quiet and my mother cried out, 'Maybe if I had a man for a husband I wouldn't need to drink.' I was ten years old and I really wasn't sure what she meant but I knew it had to do with sex and for some reason that scared me a lot, an awful lot. It scared me so much that I did something I'd done rarely before. I went to my mother and asked her what she had meant. The first time she just sort of laughed it off, and said something about little pitchers having big ears. That reaction made me wonder and made me even more scared because my mother was like my father, she didn't laugh much either. I asked her again. She got mad and told me I'd never understand, then gave me a lecture about talking about family matters with outsiders. I have to admit they were very careful about that. They never fought or yelled in front of sitters, cooks, or cleaning women. They didn't do that."

He stopped, wiped his forehead with a handkerchief as if he were sweating, which he wasn't. "Al," I said, slowly, "that line from your mother doesn't mean your father was a homosexual."

He looked away. He closed his eyes as if he were in pain. His voice, terribly controlled, told me he was. "By the time I'd finished sixth grade, she sometimes would call him a fag. Then they would have the same conversation. I have it memorized. He'd say in a scared, angry voice 'Don't call me that. Don't call me that. Albert will hear you!' And she'd say, 'So what? So what if he does? So you are ashamed then. You don't want him to know he's got a father who prefers men to women!' My father was gay."

"It bothers you a lot."

He nodded.

"Makes you wonder about your own sense of masculinity."

He nodded.

I had to ask it. "Do you feel attracted to men sexually?"

He shook his head. "No. No. I'm not, but. . . ."

"What?" I asked.

He looked down. "Doc, I can't seem to do it. . . . I don't seem to want to do it with Jill, or with any woman for that matter. I've got a very low sex drive."

"Are you impotent?"

"No, I don't think so because I can get an erection if she fondles me. Sometimes it takes a while though." He sighed. "It gets to be such a chore that we don't do it too often. She probably told you that."

I nodded. Dynamically anyway, everything seemed to be falling into place.

There was a pause for several moments.

Al gave me a hesitant look. "All of which brings me to why I came to see you."

I looked at him curiously. "What do you mean?"

"Well, my parents didn't have much of a marriage but they stayed together. I'd like to stay with my wife. I love her. You heard my story. You heard hers. Do you think we can make it?"

I shook my head. "I don't know."

"Doc, I really love Jill. I'll do anything and put up with just about anything to keep her."

He spoke almost as if he were trying to bribe me to arrange it so that Jill would stay with him. Ironically, while the begging-like quality of his tone irritated me, it also engendered a lot of sympathy. His last comment intrigued me. Was he unconsciously letting me know that he would put up with her infidelity? It was not a comment that he had thought about. It couldn't be. And it had been verbalized for himself as well as for me because this was a very jealous man, a man who hovered over his wife at parties, who reproved her and berated her for even imagined flirtations. "Al," I said in my kindest voice, "the person you need to be confiding in, sharing these thoughts with, is Jill, not me. I can't get her to stay with you. You have to do that."

"I try to talk to her," he said in a voice that made me think of an awkward adolescent.

"But," I said patiently, "I'll bet you don't. I'll bet," I said with certainty, "that she knows nothing at all about your father."

"God no!"

"Al," I said, "if she did, she might be far more understanding and tolerant about your lack of interest in sex."

He looked up. "That bothers her, eh?"

"Of course it bothers her." I didn't regret the edge to my voice.

We spent the last few minutes arranging a time for the next session, which was to include Penny and Bill as well as Jill.

Reflections

There was an incredible amount of movement in this one session—far, far more than I see in most, perhaps than in any. Al moved from a state of virtual denial to one of painful awareness.

Doing therapy one learns that ironies abound in people's lives. These ironies are of critical importance in their development and are usually at the core of their lives. They explain much of the why of it. So it is with this man.

Serious, humorless, hard working, and successful, Al is very much like his father, which he doesn't want to be because to be so, he under-

stands, might mean to be a homosexual. To date, his denial that he is much like his father, together with his refusal even to think of his dad as gay, has so bound him up emotionally that he is not able to perform sexually.

These dynamics have led to the most salient irony of Al's life—his marriage to Jill. It is a relationship that closely resembles the one his parents had. And he helped to promote it. He helped develop it.

Al's self-doubt about his masculinity tells me that he is greatly threatened by Jill's sexuality. At the same time, I do believe that he does love Jill in his way. Finally, he did come to seek help for his problems, and did ventilate and self-disclose remarkably in this session. Question: Will his love for Jill (unreturned) be enough to hold the marriage together?

At this point, I am pessimistic.

The Wentworth family was seated in the room when I opened the connecting office door. Bill, 13, and Penny, 14, flanked Jill on the couch. Al sat alone, off to their right. How families seat themselves anywhere is always informative. This is especially true for children, particularly when they are in a threatening place such as a psychotherapist's waiting room.

"Come on in, Wentworths." I nodded and greeted each of the two children as they passed me.

Jill led the parade. Al brought up the rear.

They replicated the waiting room seating, children on each side of mother, Al alone in a recliner. I took the other seat.

I had never seen either child. Both favored their mother. They had her oval face, her nose and well-formed mouth. Both, however, had Al's sandy hair. The best way to deal with children at an initial family therapy session is to let them know they are welcome, and then let them participate as the spirit moves them. My smile and greeting had let them know they were welcome. I let my gaze sweep all four, then rest on Jill. It rested on her because she did not look happy. "How is it, Jill?"

Her look spoke of irritation, if not downright anger. "I'd like to know why Penny and Bill have to be here."

The comment took me aback. I looked at both children, addressed them as much as her. "Well, whenever there are problems in a family, the whole family is affected and. . . ."

"Whatever problems Al and I have they are ours. I really don't see why we have to drag the children into our squabbles."

"Oh, mother," Penny said, "don't be crabby before we even start."

Jill glared at her, then with the same glare said to me, "Doctor, some of these problems, as you very well know, have nothing to do with the children. They have to do with Al and me, period."

I nodded agreeably. "Jill, I'm not interested in embarrassing or bringing up issues that concern you and Al personally. . . ."

Penny had a big smile on her face. "You guys talking about sex?"

I always find candor refreshing, and for some perverse reason even when it borders on embarrassing me. "To be honest with you Penny, I had a couple of items in mind that your parents and I have discussed. That was only one of them."

"Sex?" she asked.

I had the distinct feeling that Penny had said it again because she liked to hear and say the word "sex." I nodded with a grin.

She crossed her slim legs demurely and gave me a nod that I'm sure was meant to be sophisticated. "Well, I'm glad to be here because I think our family has problems."

"What problems, Penny?" I asked, my tone perfectly serious.

"Well," she said, "Daddy is just not into the family like he used to be."

Al spoke his first words. "Just what are you talking about, young lady?"

She looked at him, then cried out, "Well, it's true. You're not. When I was a baby, you used to be home for supper every night. You're not anymore. In fact, daddy, you're just not home. I feel like I have to make an appointment to see you."

Al looked at Jill angrily. "Did you put her up to this?"

Jill was smiling. "I didn't. I didn't even want her to be here. You did. You arranged it, not me. So enjoy it."

"See how they talk to each other?" wailed Penny. "They talk like that all the time. I can't stand it."

Jill turned to her daughter. "Will you please stop now!"

Penny turned to me. "Should I stop?"

I laughed. "No. Don't stop. In this group, children say whatever they want to whenever they want to."

Penny gave her mother one of those childish "ha ha" looks. Jill gave her a dirty look and Al looked on it all disapprovingly. Then Billy bawled out, "Just one, big happy family!"

Well, I thought, at least one Wentworth had a sense of humor! "Are you happy, Billy?"

He shook his head, replying seriously, "No."

"How can he be happy?" piped Penny. "How can any of us be happy? There's just no romance in this family."

I found the comment amusing, but interesting too. "What do you mean by that, Penny?"

Al interjected. "She doesn't mean anything by that. She's read so many of these trashy romance novels that she can't differentiate between life and fiction."

Jill gave him a hard look. "Why don't you let her answer?"

Al rolled his eyes toward the ceiling.

"Yes, tell us what you meant, Penny," I said.

"Well, all I meant was that our lives are boring and nothing exciting or unexpected ever happens."

Al looked at her in disgust. "My God, child, you're only 14 years old and you say you're bored?"

Jill shook her head in irritation. "Why do your questions always have to sound like accusations? A 14-year-old can be bored. Anybody can be bored."

"You're bored, mother," Penny said. "I know you are. You have to be. There's just no romance in your life. Daddy, you're just not romantic. That's the problem."

"I don't believe this conversation! I just do not believe what I am hearing," cried Al. "My 14-year-old here is talking like an opinionated advisor to the lovelorn."

Jill, who seemed to be enjoying it all, turned to her daughter. "And tell me, dear little Miss Abby, what would you suggest?"

Penny ignored her mother's obvious amusement and spoke seriously. "I really haven't thought out what you can do, mother. I just told you what I think the problem is."

What I found amazing up to this point was that this 14-year-old had instinctively, intuitively, touched upon the problem. Her mother must have pursued the same line of thinking. It was such a line that had probably led her to her affairs. All of which led me to think that Penny and Jill are very close, and that being 14 years old does not obviate being sensitive to another's feelings and needs, especially when that "other" is your mother.

Al spoke in a sarcastic tone. "So, the basic problem in this family is that I'm not romantic."

"I think so, daddy."

"Penny," he said with more than a little anger in his voice, "there's a lot more to life than romance."

The look Jill gave her husband was filled with pity. "Really?"

Poor Al didn't catch the look or the irony in her voice. "Of course there is."

"Well, Al, tell us what there is." Her tone told me that she knew exactly what he was going to say.

"There's love that comes from sacrifice, there's the concern that comes from caring, and I know it drives you nuts when I say it, but there's working hard for those you love."

Penny looked at me. "They fight about this all the time."

"If you've decided who's right, tell them, Penny." My tone was light, my intent serious.

Penny looked at her father and told him. "Daddy, you work very, very hard for us. I know that's true. You teach all day, then work all night and summers and vacations and all the time. You work so hard for us that you can't be with us. What good is it to work like that? I think mother is right, that it's just an excuse not to be with us. Daddy, I hate to tell you this, but we're getting used to being a family without you." The honesty with which she said all that was disarming.

Al gave his wife a hard, nasty look. "What do you do, coach her?"

"Oh, daddy, what a thing to say! That's not fair and it's not true either, and you know it. I live in your house but I don't really live with you because I never see you and I don't think I see you because you don't want to see me or Bill or mother."

"That is pure nonsense, young lady, and you know it."

Bill cried out again. "Nonsense, nonsense, nonsense or Penny's the name, nonsense is the game!"

At Bill's comment Al's head jerked up. He looked at his son confusedly, as if he were trying to decide whether he was being facetious or serious. His question reflected his look. "You being a smart aleck or what?"

Jill drawled, "What he's trying to do is make his no-sense-of-humor father see some humor in all this."

Al's reply was a whine. "Well I just don't see anything funny about being ganged up on."

His wife responded quickly and impatiently. "There you go again with that nobody loves me bit."

I knew Al was not close to Jill. I suspected, despite some comments he had made at our initial session about Penny being like him, that he was not close to his children either. What I had not known until now was that he felt virtually alienated from all of them. Many of these feelings were, of course, his fault, due to his own unfortunate quirks and behavior. The feelings, however, had to be compounded by the demeaning way he was treated by Jill in front of the children. As I looked at the hurt expression on his face, I wondered to what extent these feelings of hurt and alienation precipitated his constant absence from home. Then again, did he feel like a stranger because he had essentially made himself one through his workaholic schedule? I sighed inwardly as I realized these questions were all academic—

the reality was that Al acted, and quite apparently was treated, like an unwanted relative. Billy had treated him best, although facetiously. They were all looking at me with embarrassment. I felt that, and their tension too.

Then without so much as a smile Bill cried out, "End of round one!"

Nobody so much as grinned.

Al quipped, "My son, the comedian."

Jill didn't quip. She just glared at him.

Al sighed. "There's an awful lot of animosity in this family."

Penny agreed. "Yes, there is, daddy. And why do you think that is?"

"I don't know why," he said in a flat unhappy voice. "That's why I brought us here."

"When I gave my opinion before about why we've got problems you put me down. You just won't listen!"

"Penny," he said, his voice heavy and threatening, "romance has got absolutely nothing to do with anything here, believe it."

Penny got up. She shouted, "It does too, and I just can't understand how you don't see that."

Everyone looked at Jill, who looked away, an ironic smile playing at the corner of her mouth. She spoke slowly. "Al, what I think she's saying is that there's no love between you and me."

"But I do love you and you know it," he cried. Then he looked at both children and in a choked voice repeated, "I love your mother more than I love my life."

"Maybe," said Penny drily, "but not more than you love work."

Jill laughed. Billy laughed. Al did not laugh. He looked at me, then at each of them. For a split, suspended moment, I thought he was going to cry. He didn't. Suddenly the look on his face changed to one of anger. He sat up in his chair and spoke to Penny in a voice that was both harsh and resolute. "The reason we've got the problems we've got is that your mother is alcoholic."

Penny turned to Jill. The two exchanged little knowing smiles.

"So what's the big secret joke about?" he asked.

"Mother told us you would say that."

"I said it," said Al with conviction, "because it's true."

Billy spoke his first serious words, and he spoke them quietly. "Dad, I've never even seen mom drunk."

"Me neither," cried Penny.

"Neither of you would know if she was, and let's be honest, even if you knew, you wouldn't admit it."

Penny answered in her high-pitched cry, "We'd know if she was drunk and we'd admit it." She looked toward Billy for confirmation.

Bill nodded. "Sure, why not? Why lie about it?"

Jill's look was one of pride. It said, 'The children are mine.'

I speak as little as possible at family sessions, preferring to observe dynamics and alliances between and among family members. In some families, these are difficult to ascertain. In this one, they were transparent and the whys were obvious. Not only were the children in Jill's corner physically and emotionally, but Al's whole style with them seemed bent on keeping them at a distance. He spoke down to them rather than to them, or he spoke angrily, or, worse still, he retreated into a defensive stance that was more childish than any either of his children had yet displayed. To help him out a little, I thought it might be well to see if I could get him to self-disclose about his own childhood. "Al," I said, "why don't you tell Penny and Billy why it's so easy to deny a parent's alcoholism?"

He gave me the same confused look he'd given Bill earlier, only this one said even more plainly, "Whose side are you on anyway?" However, my message got through. "O.K.," he said. "You're probably right. The time's come when maybe I should talk about my own mother."

"What about your mother?" Billy asked.

"She was alcoholic," he said with embarrassment.

"What's that got to do with my mother being alcoholic," asked Penny in a contrary tone.

The embarrassment in Al's voice had spread to his face. "Well," he said, "I can tell the symptoms."

Jill shot him a dirty look, then moved the look to me. "Are you going to let this foolishness continue?"

My question had not moved the talk in the direction I had intended. Again I intervened. "What I had hoped, Al, was that you might share with your family some of the stuff we talked about before, about your mother and how she was just not very loving."

Al nodded and started telling some of what he had discussed with me about how his mother, isolated in her darkened bedroom, smelled of eucalyptus cough drops and gin. He started out slowly, self-consciously, but before he was done, he was speaking from the heart. What he had said was very effective. I could see by the expressions on their faces that all three of his family were moved.

Penny got up and hugged him. "I never knew any of that stuff, daddy. It really does help me understand better."

"Yeah, me too," agreed Billy. "But dad, and no offense, how does all that make mom alcoholic?"

At that moment I felt the Wentworths were at some kind of important emotional juncture. If Al could back off from his strong need to see Jill as alcoholic (I was convinced now that she was not), there would be far more hope for the development of a closer, more honest relationship between them. More important, he would let his children get closer to him because then all three would have a more comparable view of Jill.

But Al could not back off. The condescension returned to his voice. "There are things I just can't discuss here with you kids. It's too personal. It's like she said herself when we first started, it's really between us."

Jill, who had been quiet for a while, exploded. "That is a cop-out and you know it! I don't know what's so personal between us that makes you think I'm alcoholic. Alcoholism infects kids growing up. It infected you and it infected me. It infected our judgment about people. That's probably why," she said with sudden irony, "we married each other. It devastated my self-esteem. All that. I admit to it. But damn it, I'm not alcoholic."

Her voice a mixture of sorrow and curiosity, Penny asked Al. "Why do you keep saying she's alcoholic?"

I knew why but I couldn't say it. To do so would probably alienate him and engender hostility in the kids, and even more in Jill. As I suspected, Jill also knew why.

She verbalized it. "He keeps saying it because it makes him feel more important than me."

"Is that true, daddy?" Penny asked.

Al snapped his reply. "No, it doesn't make me feel important. It only makes me feel ashamed."

Billy's eyes widened, "You're ashamed of mom?"

"I didn't say that I'm ashamed of her," he replied quickly, "just of her alcoholic ways."

Both children looked bewildered, and Penny a little angry too. "Daddy," she said, "you are really out of it. What you're saying is you are ashamed of something she's not. That's crazy."

"Penny, those words hurt, really hurt. Here I express an honest opinion and you call me crazy."

"Hurt," she cried. "You talk about hurt. Just imagine how you hurt mother. And how you hurt Billy and me."

Al's surprise as usual was, if nothing else, honest. "How did I, what did I say or do to hurt you and Billy?"

"Daddy, she is our mother. And all you seem to want to do, all you do, is put her down! How do you think that makes us feel? We are her children!"

I'd thought the moment a dramatic one, a tense one, yet Billy actually laughed. "Yeah, dad, meet mom's children."

Al's last comments and honest surprise about the effect on his children convinced me that he had little appreciation of their sentiments and needs. Apparently he didn't see that their feelings were with their mother. His denial of that fact kept him emotionally out of tune with them, and with Jill also. Essentially what he had done in these last few minutes was to reinforce the basic view expressed by Penny, but which all three had of him—that he was 'out of it'!

The session had deteriorated to the point where both children were now berating Al. That could lead to no good at all. I decided to intervene by changing the topic. I addressed the children. "You know, I know all about your parents but I really don't know much about you two." Actually, the one I really wanted to know about was Billy. His dynamics were not as apparent to me as were Penny's.

"What do you want to know?" asked Penny.

I shrugged. "Let's start with school. You like it?"

"Not very much. It's work."

Jill smiled proudly. "She does very well. She's an honor student."

"I work hard," said Penny.

"Penny's the name, A's are the game," Billy said with a smile on his face.

"What about you, Billy?" I asked.

He shrugged.

"Billy's a clown," Penny said, "at home and in school." She mimicked her brother. "Billy's the name, making fun is the game."

"I'm not what the teachers call a serious student." He said "serious student" in a deep, deep voice.

"Billy's smarter than I am. He's just not interested in school." She looked at her brother. "Right?"

Billy shrugged. "Who knows?"

During the remaining few moments, we focused on the children. What I heard reinforced what I had learned about them. They were close and liked each other but were very different. She was serious, hard working, and very much concerned with success and achievement. In these traits, she was a kind of female Al. Al told her, almost gleefully, "Like it or not, you take after me." Penny, who had been talking, went on as if he had not said it. Jill glared at him, and Bill, I noticed, had put on a wistful, vulnerable look, one that was totally out of character. It intrigued me, as did Billy generally. He was quite unlike his father, appearing to have none of Al's more evident traits and displaying a humorous aspect that I'd not seen in any of the other Wentworths. I needed to think more about the meaning of this.

We finished the session, and at Al's request made an appointment for the following Wednesday. This one is to be with Al and Jill only. Jill, while she agreed to it, did not seem especially pleased.

Reflections

At this point I wonder seriously if the marriage can be saved. There are major obstacles. The first is Al himself. My sense now is that, consciously or unconsciously, his interest in its salvation is at best only half-hearted. I think this because he likes to be away from his family and/or is afraid to be with them. Regardless of the reason, the effect is the same— he is not with them physically or emotionally, and as Penny pointed out, they are learning to function as a family without him. My hope is that his self-disclosures regarding his mother will help to alleviate some of the threat he feels, especially from Jill. If this threat is alleviated, his denial will abate and he should become more attuned emotionally to all of them.

The second major obstacle is, of course, Jill, who continues to display few, if any, positive feelings toward her husband. Add to that the fact that she needs to be in an affair in order to stay away from drinking and the problems with saving the marriage seem formidable indeed. This session showed Jill to have some positive and healthy qualities, the most salient of which is her lack of denial, rare for the adult child of an alcoholic. In addition, she is close to both of her children, especially to her daughter.

Penny is much like her in emotional astuteness and in her way of relating. It is interesting to note that she is also much identified with her father whom, ironically, she perceives in the same negative light as does Jill.

The enigma is Billy. He appears to be growing up quite unlike either parent. I'm concerned about him, and Penny too. Reared by two children of alcoholics, they live in a climate of emotional turmoil, with much that is abnormal and dishonest and with little that is sane and true. Climate notwithstanding, both children function relatively well. This is a tribute to Jill's competence as a person and as a mother.

Despite their apparent health, I have qualms and questions about their ability to make and develop good and meaningful relationships in future years. Question: What can Penny be learning about what a man is and does? I ask that because she seems to have so little respect for her father. At the same time, as noted, she is much identified with him. A speculative point, important too. Is Penny structuring for a lot of self-hate when she becomes an adult?

Obviously, Billy has learned little, if anything, that is enhancing about men from his father. But what is he learning about women from his mother? Has he learned that they are more important than men? That they are stronger than men? That they are to be feared because they berate, demean, and control relationships?

In most families, there is one person toward whom the members look for direction and security. In this family, it is Jill. She is the key. Should she elect to give up her affairs, I believe she could effect healthful changes for the whole family. She has the strength to do so. She could make the marriage work. On the other hand, should she elect to stay in the marriage and continue the status quo, I'm convinced that all the Wentworths will suffer in their relationships with others, and with each other.

On the following Wednesday, Jill arrived alone. "He said he'd meet me here. Did he call or anything?" she asked.

I shook my head. "No."

"Figures," she said. Her lip curled in disgust.

"Jill, you know him better than I do. Will he show up?"

She shrugged. "I really don't know, and I've reached that point where I really don't care."

"What happened?"

She smiled at my evident interest. "Nothing dramatic. But all week I've been mulling over what I discovered here last week. Well, I didn't exactly discover it. I guess I knew it all along but it really didn't all hit me until she started talking about romance."

"You're talking about Penny?"

"Yes, Penny. How much," she said with more than a little awe, "how much she thinks like me, how much she really is like me."

The awe made me curious. "How does that make you feel?"

She looked at me, then looked away and spoke in a small voice. "Scared. It makes me feel scared."

Her reply surprised me. "What scares you?"

"I've short-changed her. I've created the same kind of home for her that my parents raised me in. And if she gets married, she's going to end up just like me, in a loveless marriage."

"But the reality is that she is not you, and more important, you must have done some things right. She seems so healthy, so alive!"

Jill gave me a wan little smile. "Yeah, she seems like that but the truth is she's a lonely little girl. She has no friends. She puts up a good front, but it's only a front. Behind that front beats the heart of a scared little girl. Believe me, I know."

I believed her. It all fit with my thoughts after the family session. What surprised me was what she had not said. "What about Billy," I asked, "how do you see him?"

"Billy," she said, shaking her head, "is a mystery to me. I've always loved him, hugged him, cooed and gooed him as a little baby, but he was always a little distant. By the time he was five, he never came around much for attention, not even if he got hurt playing." She shrugged "I don't know, maybe it's because he's male. They," she said with a loud chuckle, "have always been a complete mystery. Look what I chose for a husband!"

For several minutes I had had the feeling that she was vacillating about telling me something. I broached this feeling gently. "You've been thinking a lot about you and your kids. Have you thought, no not thought, have you decided anything?"

At that point, there was a loud knock at the door, and before I could say "just a moment" or "come in," it burst open. Red faced and out of breath, Al cried out his apology, "I'm sorry I'm late!"

My first reaction was irritation. Jill had been about to answer my question. That answer was now lost, at least for a while. The poor boob did not even know how to enter a room! I wiped the irritation off my face, indicated with a nod that he should close the door, and waved him to the recliner opposite the two of us.

Jill shook her head. "Good-sized deal cooking, eh?" Though framed as a question, it came out as a statement, dripping in sarcasm.

For once Al felt and heard the tone. "As a matter of fact, yes, it is a big deal," he said stiffly.

"You must do pretty well selling real estate," I said. I said it because I wanted his reaction. He had never seemed a salesman to me. Indeed, more than once I had wondered how someone so utterly unattuned to people could be effective as a salesman.

"I do," he beamed. "Made double my teacher's salary last year."

"And you spent double the amount of time, too," observed Jill drily.

He ignored his wife's comment and continued proudly. "I sold over a million dollars worth of real estate this year. I don't do it just for the money, although," he winked at me, "I wouldn't do it if there wasn't money. But really it's the people, doctor, the people. They really grab me. Meet new people all the time. Love it. Just love it."

As I listened to his words—effusive but sincere—I thought, so much for having to be attuned to people to sell real estate. I replied weakly but with all the sincerity I could muster. "I'm glad for you, Al."

"Now, how's it going here?" he asked.

I replied honestly. "I'm not sure. How is it going, Jill?"

She looked at Al. "I'm so glad you made it tonight." The sudden frankness and gentleness in her voice, so unusual when addressing her husband, made me sit up.

He gave her a little nod, apparently happy he had pleased her, probably even happier that she had spoken decently to him. "I'm glad too, hon." He looked at me. "It's good to be here, really is."

I fished for the lost answer to my question that intuition told me had something to do with why Jill had spoken so civilly to Al. "Why are you so glad that Al made it here for this session, Jill?"

"It could be because she really loves me," Al said.

Several seconds passed before I realized that this was Al's attempt at being funny.

I smiled, albeit thinly. Jill just ignored it.

"Al," she said, looking unhappy, "where do you think we're going?"

"What?" he asked, shifting in his seat.

She became more specific. "How do you think our marriage is going?"

"Well, it's not going the best but that's why we're here, to see if we can make it go better, to see if we can improve it."

The unhappy look still fixed, she asked, "Do you really think it can be improved?"

"Of course it can," he said, a little too loudly.

There was a pause.

I let my intuition ask the question that would advance what I thought Jill was trying to say. "Al, do you feel things have become better since our first meeting six weeks ago?"

Al nodded, a happy look on his face. "Absolutely. I see it in Jill, in the kids. We're all getting along better."

Jill shook her head. "How?" Even though it was a question, there was no curiosity in her tone, only ice.

Al's response was to look flustered. "Well, we don't fight or anything. I don't know, seems to me you've been very nice. The kids seem to be getting along well. I mean, what can I say?"

"Al," she said, "we haven't had a fight in a long, long time because I don't care to fight. The simple, awful truth is that I don't care about anything in our relationship. And the kids are the same as ever. They've never given us problems but they are lonely and unhappy because they are living in a house where there is no love, or what Penny calls romance."

"Oh God," wailed Al, "we're back to that!"

"Yeah," she said, "we're back to that. Back to square one."

I addressed my words to Jill, hoping Al would tune in to what she had just said. "You don't feel things are any better?"

Jill shook her head. "Not even a little bit."

"But damn it," cried Al, "am I crazy? I know you've been treating me really nice for I don't know how long. I really enjoy talking to you on the phone at supper time. You ask me what I want for a snack when I come home, and it's all there on the stove waiting for me. I mean, all that's got to mean something."

I knew what it all meant. Jill had told me at our last session together. It was precisely this hypocritical meaning of her "nice" behavior to Al that I sensed strongly Jill had wanted to discuss just before he had arrived. She looked a little embarrassed or scared as she searched for a way to address that meaning. "Sometimes," I said not speaking directly to either one, "we act nice so that we don't have to deal with the problem."

"True," said Jill.

"What are you two talking about?" asked Al.

I saw Jill take a deep breath.

"Al," she said, "we don't have a marriage. The most we have is an unhappy alliance."

"Of course we have a marriage. We were married, married in a church."

"But we're not living as husband and wife. We're living like brother and sister, and a brother and sister who don't like each other."

"I like you," he cried quickly. "In fact, I love you."

Jill's look of embarrassment of a few moments ago had dissipated. Now she looked as though she was trying to control anger. "Al," she said evenly, "I can't say that I don't like you because that wouldn't be true. You're not a bad person. Certainly you're not one that many people could dislike. . . ."

"Thanks," he cried, "thanks for the crumb and the left-handed compliment."

Jill shrugged. "I'm sorry. I'm certainly not interested in hurting you, Al, but get this straight." She paused as she leaned toward him, eyes leveled into his. "I do not love you. I never have, and I swear to God I don't think I ever can."

Even for Al the reaction was remarkable. A little grin had appeared on his face. He nodded and gazed at his wife, not so much in anger or hurt, as with a look of tolerance and understanding. "I've known that for a long time, that you're not exactly crazy about me, Jill, but that's O.K. We get along. My parents weren't crazy about each other but they got along too, although not exactly ginger-peachy, but they got along and stayed married. And," he said resolutely, "we will too."

Jill's embarrassment, like her anger, had dissipated. Only a sadness remained, "Al, that's what I'm saying to you. I don't want to stay married to you."

Al, who had been leaning forward in his recliner, fell back hard. He started to speak, but his jaw went slack. Only a little gurgle came out.

"I am sorry, but I want a divorce," she said hoarsely.

Suddenly he sat up again. "But why? Why? I support you completely. You have everything you could possibly want. You don't even have to work."

"Al," she said, "we've gone all over that before. I'm not going to again. The bottom line is that I don't love you. Our marriage is a farce.

We sleep in the same bed and we never even touch each other. The truth is, I'm frigid with you and you don't seem to be able to. I read something once that seems very true for us, 'Bodies don't lie.' "

"Are you saying you want to get a divorce because we don't have sex? Is that what you're saying?"

"Not just because of that. That's not the most important thing, but it is important to me."

Al's face assumed the perplexed look that had become almost familiar. "It's important to you?"

She nodded.

"I swear I didn't know that, Jill."

I believed it.

Jill did too. "I know," she said. She said it with pity, I thought.

"Jill, it isn't that I'm having or ever had an affair. I mean there's no one else, never has been, and I can tell you there never will be."

Despite the gravity of the moment, those words and the earnestness with which Al had delivered them for some reason made me want to laugh.

Jill must have felt the same way because she grinned. She opened her mouth and for an awful second I had the feeling she was going to say, "Christ, who'd ever want to!" She didn't, only murmured a gentle, "I know, Al. I know you're faithful."

"Well, then, why can't we stay married?" he asked brightly.

The question made me think that Al might be, unconsciously but deliberately, pushing her to bludgeon him with the news of her affairs. It might very well be the only way he knew to confront her, to bring the whole thing to a head.

My thought proved prophetic. Jill made an exasperated sound and told him. "Because I can't be faithful to you."

"What do you mean?" he asked weakly.

"Just that."

"You mean you're having an affair?"

Given Al's incredible denial system, I really expected his question to be couched in astonishment. There wasn't any, which meant that my initial surmise had been correct at some level and that he had either known, or had at least suspected strongly.

"Yes, Al, I'm having an affair."

There was a long pause. Al looked at me and suddenly I felt that he was going to say something magnanimous like, "Well. We all make mistakes and I forgive you, Jill." He didn't do that. Instead he said something far more typical and normal, except that he didn't say it, but croaked it, as if he were holding back tears. "I don't know what to say."

Jill reached for a tissue and began to dab at her eyes. "Nothing to say."

"Who is it?" he asked.

"Doesn't matter," she said.

Al's response came out as a roar. "It doesn't matter! Here you are screwing around with some guy and you tell me it doesn't matter. Who is it!"

The roar made both Jill and me jump. Jill recovered instantly, however, apparently preferring an angry reaction to a meek one. "No it doesn't, because he's not the first."

Al literally turned white. "He's not the first?"

"No."

Years of living with Al must have engendered a tremendous amount of hostility because my distinct impression was that Jill enjoyed saying that "no." I knew what she was going to say now, and I agreed with it even though it seemed unkind. She had to do it to tear down the thick wall of denial behind which he had isolated himself precisely not to know.

Al's next words confirmed all my impressions about the dynamics of their unfortunate relationship. "Don't bother to tell me anymore. I don't want to know."

"Too damned bad," she cried, "because you are going to know, like it or not."

Then, like a little child, he turned a pleading look to me. Even as I said them, I realized that they were the first words I had spoken in quite a few minutes. "Al," I said in my most empathic voice, "what Jill wants to do is tell you why she's had these affairs. Painful as it may seem, better to know than not to know. Then if she goes through with the divorce, maybe you'll know better why and how it all came about." How much of all that he could understand and accept I didn't know, but he nodded.

"You've got to know," she said "because I've got to tell you and I've got to tell you to preserve my own sense of dignity."

She told him that she had to have the affairs to escape the boredom and the loneliness of her life, and the inattention. She spoke of her emotionally deprived childhood and related how he had brought the horror of it all back with that inattention. "And so I went out and found another man, three other men to be exact."

Throughout her explanation, Al had sat meekly, head down like a little boy being lectured by his mother or his teacher. When she finished, he said, "Now that you've told me, can we get on with our lives?"

"My God, Al," she cried, "you really didn't understand anything I told you."

"But I did," he yelled, "and I'm telling you I forgive you. That's how much I love you."

"I don't want your forgiveness," she screamed. "I want a divorce." Tears in her eyes, she told him. "What I've done was wrong, I know that. Believe it or not, I did it to keep my sanity. But what I'm realizing is that I'm becoming promiscuous. And I am not going to do this! I want a relationship in which I can give love and get love."

Al's eyes lit up. "Christ, me too!"

She shook her head firmly. "Not with you! No way."

There was a long pause.

"The real reason we've got to get a divorce," she said slowly, "is because of the children."

Al gave her a condescending look. "You've really gone off the deep end, you know that! Everyone knows divorce devastates kids."

"Maybe," she said, "but I think that this marriage will do it faster than any divorce. Don't you see? Don't you see that we've created a home where our kids are learning to live with lies, exactly the way you and I did growing up? I don't love you, and you don't even know what love is, and we live together. You know what that's telling them? That's telling them we are liars, or at least that it's O.K. to live a lie. And," she screamed, "if it isn't telling them that, it's telling them that we are all screwed up." She fell back.

Al's condescending look turned to one of scorn. "You've got some nerve telling me about being a liar and living a lie and being all screwed up and all the while you've been screwing around, and for four or five years. Jesus! Talk about a liar, a screwed-up liar, and a hypocrite too!"

For some reason, in that one moment my intuition was that Al finally felt her peer. It was the only time in all of our sessions that I'd had that feeling. It had to be because of the guilt she had admitted to for her affairs. How sad, I thought. Only when he knew she felt guilty was he able to feel on a par with her!

I told them that our session was about over and asked them if they wanted another appointment. Al gave me a sarcastic grin that told me no and that he felt I had failed to save his marriage. Jill declined but said she would be in touch.

At the door, Al spoke to her with contempt, "You really think you're going to be able to hack it on your own?"

A vulnerable look flitted across her face, but it didn't stay. She looked at me a moment, then turned to Al, "I really don't know," she said, "but I'm going to give it a try."

On that they left.

Reflections

In retrospect it is obvious that this marriage was doomed at the outset. Its premise was not the solid realities of love or affection but a distortion of reality through denial. What is truly remarkable about it is that it lasted 15 years. However, it did last because for over a decade Jill was able to deny its loveless nature and because she was too afraid to attempt to live life independently.

Her human need for attention served as the catalyst to finally effect the dissolution of the denial. Nevertheless, I believe that her fear of coping with life on her own would have kept her in the marriage.

Penny's belief and analysis that the familial problems stemmed from Jill's need for "romance" rocked Jill, made her fully conscious of what she already knew dimly, namely, that she was structuring disaster for Penny's future relationships, and those of her son too.

She talked also about not wanting to be promiscuous, about wanting a relationship in which she could give and get love. Although I believe that, my conviction is that had she not been so finely attuned to her children's needs, had she not had such a strong conscience about their future relationships; the affair would probably have been enough to fill her personal needs for attention and closeness.

Everything considered, I believe she is probably doing the right thing in seeking a divorce. Then again, Jill is the child of an alcoholic and as such, she may vacillate or procrastinate for years.

It will be interesting to see if she follows through.

Epilogue

I was never to see Al again. However, Jill called me about three weeks after our last appointment to say that she had filed for divorce. "I did it the day after our last appointment," she said, almost cheerfully.

"How are you feeling about it now?" I asked.

"Still scared," she replied, "but I'm handling it." "Al," she continued, "has been a perfect darling about helping out even though he was mad about moving out. He sends money every other day. He even had a checking account made out in my name and deposited money in it. I paid my first bills this week."

Almost a year passed before I had contact with Jill again. I met her at a fast-food restaurant on an afternoon when I was having a late lunch. She gave me a big "Hi" and a bigger smile, and sat at my table with her hamburger and soft drink. The red burgundy suit contrasted well with her black hair and white skin.

"I need this hamburger," she said, "because I had no lunch and I won't get home until after seven tonight."

"You're working?" I asked.

Her eyes widened in realization. "Of course, I never told you. I did mean to but I've been so busy," she said happily. She told me she was selling real estate. "And guess who got me the job."

"Al?"

"Right! You know," she said, lowering her voice, "I never knew making money could be so easy."

I smiled. She almost sounded like her former husband.

"He's been so good about his alimony payments. I get them almost a week before they're due with a note asking me to let him know if I need anything. Funny," she said, "we live in the same town, and although he doesn't seem bitter at all, I never see him. Kids don't either. I guess he prefers it that way." She gave the impression that her children were still lonely.

"Sounds like you are coping pretty well," I said.

"I feel good," she said, "because my life is honest now. I'm not dating anyone and I don't want to right now, but I will when I'm ready." She sounded confident and relaxed about that.

Walking back to my office I thought about what she had said about Al and his behavior. In some ways I concluded that the divorce was a relief for him. In losing Jill he may have lost a status symbol but apparently he had found relief too, relief from all the emotional obligations imposed by being a husband and a father. I nodded to myself. Al probably liked being legally divorced from his family since he had been emotionally divorced from them anyway.

Almost four years after I had last seen them, I contacted the four Wentworths for permission to tell their story. Not long after that, I received a note from Jill telling me she had remarried almost two years before. It ended with these lines.

"I found out that loving your mate is a fantastic investment. It's a little like buying an apartment house at the beginning of a housing boom. You get to keep all you put into it, then you get fabulous dividends, and besides all that, your investment appreciates incredibly!"

6

THE DO'S AND DON'TS OF ENHANCEMENT

The Do's for Both ACOA and Friend

The basic message of this book is that adult children of alcoholics are what they are because they were reared in an environment that was emotionally depriving and stultifying. The environment may have been an explosive one, in which tempers flared sporadically, and fights broke out suddenly and unexpectedly. But the environment could just as easily have been at the opposite end of the emotional continuum, where nothing ever happened—an environment characterized by boredom and indifference, where communication of any kind was at a premium. The effects of both environments are the same in that they promote feelings of insecurity, of not being loved, and of low self-esteem. These same effects, in turn, inculcate into these adult children the emotional conviction that their love has little worth and that they are not worthy of anyone else's. It is for this reason that adult children of alcoholics find the giving and taking of love a bewildering, frightening process, often a veritable mystery.

Too often, these core feelings of insecurity and incompetence with love and a low self-esteem foster a crippling view of self and a distorted view of others. It is for these reasons that if adult children are able to form relationships, these are short-lived, superficial, and usually demeaning both for them and the other person. Invariably such relationships fail.

These same core traits spawn a variety of personality characteristics that facilitate and structure for these unhappy relationships. These characteristics are common among adult children and make them feel different from others. Among the most salient ones noted in the preceding stories were (1) an inability to trust, (2) unreliability, (3) a cavalier attitude toward the truth, (4) an attraction to pain, (5) vacillation, (6) preoccupation with self, and (7) an inability to make commitments, whether emotional, social, or professional.

If you are the adult child of an alcoholic (ACOA), you should know that it is precisely because you harbor one or more of these characteristics that you have had to suffer unhappy, even destructive, relationships in the past. The following guidelines should help you to alleviate the unhappiness in some and obviate those that could prove destructive.

If you are the friend of an ACOA, these guidelines not only should help you to avoid problems with the relationship but should help you to enhance it.

The Do's for Both ACOA and Friend

Do be aware of who you are. By that I mean you should have a full appreciation of where you're coming from, specifically that you were indeed reared in an alcoholic home and *what* all that *means* about what you came to understand about yourself. Being aware of who you are has to do also with a full appreciation of your rights and your ability to make choices now for your future.

Do seek help. As an adult child, be fully appreciative that there is much help available to you, that there are many groups, agencies, and institutions that are ready to help you learn and grow precisely because you were reared in an alcoholic home. Alcoholics Anonymous, Al-Anon, and the relatively new ACOA groups provide both individual and group counseling. They are listed in your local telephone directory.

Do perceive each other realistically. How you view each other will determine how a relationship will proceed. You need to be cognizant of the dynamics in which both of you were reared. A critically important aspect of your perception is to *differentiate* and *discriminate* between person and behavior. Bear in mind that finally all of you are more than your irritating or even destructive traits and more important, both of you do need to seek to overcome them. Bear in mind, too, that understanding and kindness can help do this. Blame and condemnation usually only reinforce those qualities you find irritating or believe can be destructive. Most important, if you both want your relationship to endure, your view of each other has to be as *peers*. That is, you have to see yourselves as equals. Neither can have more status than the other in either's eyes. The "give and take" notion is O.K., provided both do both some of the time and neither gives nor takes all of the time. Enhancement for each and endurance of the relationship lie in the notion that control of the relationship is in the hands and hearts of both.

Do communicate. Your talk and interaction should be aimed at only one goal, and that constantly—namely, communication. Communication between the two of you can occur on three levels: the verbal, the emotional, and the behavioral. When all three levels jibe, this happens because your words ride on appropriate emotion and fit your facial expression. Such messages are honest, dispel suspicion, and make for communication. There is no communication when the words do not jibe with the emotion or the facial or body expression; i.e., when the words are "I love you" but the tone is "get off my back." Such a message is at best mixed, if not dishonest, and can engender suspicion and anger. It certainly does not make for communication.

Do be flexible with each other. Recognize that absolute positions have no place in human relationships because they can never work. Know that an arbitrary view of self or of your friend can never enhance but can structure for disappointment. The simple reality is that you are both human, and you both can and will make mistakes. Know that mistakes do not mean failure, but only reflect the natural process of human experience. Failure can occur only when you want to discontinue the process of movement toward being the best that you can be. Flexibility on the part of both permits that process to continue indefinitely, thereby structuring for mutual growth.

Do make decisions out of choice, not guilt. Decisions, whether for one of you or for both, and whether made alone or mutually, should always be made out of choice. Decisions made because of guilt are, by definition, not freely made. Too often, the one making the decision comes to regret it and feels resentful. Invariably the effect is to structure for problems in the relationship.

If you want your relationship to be meaningful and to endure, you both must demonstrate your love and each must accept the other's love. If you are both able to do this, the relationship will enhance both of you. The miracle of love is that the one giving love is enhanced as much as the one receiving it. If you are the adult child, know that you need only communicate your desire to love and be loved. A loving friend is one who understands and is tolerant of the trauma and deprivation of your background. My recommendation is to talk and love over it.

The Don'ts

If you, the ACOA, and you, the friend, truly do want to enhance the relationship, there are certain behaviors in which you should not engage.

Do not impugn each other's motives. You impugn when you analyze, interpret, or question what the other does or says. Such behavior is premised upon suspicion and only engenders the same. When you impugn the other's motives, what you do is communicate a sense of distrust. It is an excellent and effective way to torpedo a relationship.

Do not be unreliable. Unreliability never promotes love and trust. It can, however, easily bring about resentment and frustration. It saps tolerance and understanding. Its only possible effect is to undermine the relationship.

Do not lie. A cavalier attitude toward truth is the best way I know to destroy your relationship. If you should tell an untruth, correct it. It is never too late to do so. If you tell one unknowingly and are questioned, admit to it. Lies are the strands that make up the proverbial tangled webs of deception. There is no faster way to eviscerate the substance of a relationship than to lie. Remember, once your friend finds you've lied, he/she will be hard pressed to trust you. If you want the relationship, don't lie.

Don't vacillate. People vacillate because they are afraid or are convinced that they're going to do the wrong thing. You won't have to if you remember a few simple truths: No one ever knew how good or bad a decision was until after he/she had made it. If you do err, you are in the best human tradition. Any error can be rectified, and if it can't be, the sun will continue to rise.

Don't avoid commitments. Making a commitment is the first step in the expression of love. When you make commitments, you put yourself under obligation. If you are an ACOA, this is often frightening because you are emotionally convinced that you won't be able to meet or fulfill the obligation, whatever it may be. Take a moment to realize what is obvious to everyone else; if you avoid the commitment, you will never fulfill the other's expectation. More important, you can only hurt, irritate, and alienate the other person, and you will continue to hate yourself and your life will go on unhappily. You can break the pattern only by making the commitment, scary as that may seem. Finally, you should know that as is true with most human activity, the more commitments you make, the easier it becomes to make them.

Don't overprotect. When you overprotect, you are taking a condescending view of the other person. You are saying that that person can't cope with life on his/her own because of deficiencies in the person's makeup. When you overprotect, you not only do not permit the person to grow, but you facilitate regression toward immaturity. When you overprotect, you demean yourself as well as the other person because then you become the caretaker of a neurotic baby rather than the peer of a healthy adult.

Do not be a therapist. People in a meaningful relationship can never be effective therapists for the other, because they are very much a part of the dynamics they try to treat. The reality is that no person, however loving and well intentioned, can be insightful about his or her dynamics in relation to the other person. Even more important, if you take on the role of therapist, sickness becomes an important aspect of the relationship. It necessarily becomes a central topic of talk, thought, and reflection for both of you. Adding a psychotherapeutic component to your relationship can only intellectualize it. Such a component cannot warm or personalize a relationship but it can most certainly weaken it.

ABOUT THE AUTHOR

Joseph F. Perez, Ph.D., is Professor of Psychology at Westfield State College in Massachusetts. His courses include seminars in the dynamics of alcoholism and he directs workshops for in-service professionals on techniques for counseling the alcoholic. Dr. Perez is in private practice in Northampton, Mass. He has published extensively.